BARCELONA

Like a Local

BARCELONA
Like a Local

BY THE PEOPLE WHO CALL IT HOME

Contents

NIGHTLIFE

OUTDOORS

meet the locals

HARRI DAVIES
Writer Harri left Britain for Barna for a year, and ended up staying for five. They're happiest when dancing the night away and taking a dip in the sea.

TERESA GOTTEIN MARTÍNEZ
Austrian-born journalist Teresa was seven when she moved to Spain. Living between London and Barna, she loves meeting her pals in Gràcia.

THOM LAMPON-MASTERS
Thom moved to the city ten years ago to learn the lingo. He spends his days stumbling between dive bars and bookshops, all while making the most of his linguistic skills as a translator.

SOFÌA ROBLEDO
When writer and Barcelona native Sofia isn't scribbling away in the library (her favourite place), she's hiking in the Collserola hills.

SAM ZUCKER
American travel writer, photographer and pro chef Sam enjoys exploring the city with his young daughter. Oh, and inline skating, his new hobby.

Barcelona

WELCOME TO THE CITY

Barcelona has long been a rebel. Here artists and architects break new ground, writers pen pointed literature and queer artists perform loudly and proudly. Perhaps most famously, though, Barcelona has been (and continues to be) the bastion in the fight for Catalan independence. Even today, almost a century after the Civil War, the city spurns the Spanish flag, seeing it as a symbol of anti-Catalan and fascist dictator Franco.

Yes, Barna (take note: Barça is the football club) is a complex city. It's a place of bubbling tension and fierce unity; a paradox of beauty and grime, tradition and modernity. And it's these wonderful contradictions that make Barcelonans so incredibly proud of their beloved city. And why shouldn't they be? Just look around. LGBTQ+ bars sit next door to Gothic churches, cycle lanes wind around *Modernista* mansions, vintage markets pop up in the foyers of old train stations and ultra-modern art galleries stand in medieval palaces.

No wonder, then, that Barcelonans get annoyed by *guiris* (a scathing name for tourists) who think Barna is just sea, sand and sangria. And that's exactly why you need this book – to show you what really makes Barcelona the fierce and fabled city that it is. We'll show you the vermouth bars where locals have been mingling for decades, the nightclubs that are definitely worth staying up late for (we really do mean late) and the very best spots to *tapear* (go for tapas). Of course, we can't capture every local's version of Barcelona, but we can offer a taste of the city's infectious spirit.

So, whether you're a visitor looking to go beyond the stereotypes, or a local in need of fresh inspiration, this book is here to help. Don't be a *guiri* – visit Barcelona the local way.

Liked by the locals

If you try to describe Barcelona, your words will change like a kaleidoscope: one second, the city is a cosmopolitan metropolis, the next moment, it's steeped in traditions. That's what I love most about it – there's always a different side to unearth.

THOM LAMPON-MASTERS,
WRITER AND TRANSLATOR

Hedonistic festivals in summer, age-old traditions in autumn and merry-making fun in winter: there's always something afoot in this transgressive city.

Barcelona
THROUGH THE YEAR

SPRING

TIME ON THE TERRACES
As the weather starts to warm up, crowds flood back to Barna's plentiful outdoor terraces to while away afternoons with friends.

SANT JORDI
On 23 April, the day of Catalonia's patron saint (Sant Jordi, or St George), booksellers take over the city streets and locals exchange roses and books with their loved ones.

NIGHT AT THE MUSEUM
A free dose of culture tempts Barcelonans on International Museums Day in May, with institutions staying open late into the night.

SUMMER

FESTES MAJORS
Locals love a summertime street party. Every *barri* has its own but Festes de Gràcia draws the biggest crowds of Barcelonans thanks to its incredible handmade street decorations.

SUMMER SWIMS
In summer, the days are hot and the nights are long. So, after a hard day's work, friends and families make their way to the beach for a refreshing dip and sundowner or two.

FESTIVAL FUN
Barcelona stages more music festivals than any one person's wallet (or liver) could possibly cope with. Throngs of

revellers dance the night away at the likes of Primavera Sound, Sónar, Vida and Cruïlla – to name but a few.

THE AUGUST ADÉU

Barna reaches melting point in August. Businesses work shorter hours, or shut altogether, and locals flee the sweltering city to travel or visit family in cooler climes.

AUTUMN

FALL FORAGING

As the nights draw in, friends spend their Saturdays hiking in the mountains, looking out for mushrooms, before heading home to cook up a feast.

LA MERCÈ

Barcelonans can't get enough of September's La Mercè, the city's annual festival. It's a week of *castells* (human towers), *gegants* (giant parading figures) and the traditional *correfoc* (fire run).

LA CASTANYADA

Nothing says autumn in Barna like the smell of chestnuts roasting over hot coals. On 31 October, locals eat *panellets* (marzipan cakes coated in nuts) washed down with sweet wine.

This tradition dates back centuries, when bell-ringers would eat chestnuts while pealing for the dead.

WINTER

COSY CAFÉ VISITS

As things cool off, Barcelonans gravitate toward the city's *xocolateries* for warming mugs of thick, gloopy hot chocolate.

CHRISTMAS IN THE CITY

December is a blur of work lunches and nights out with pals before the main event: Christmas Day. Catalans get together with family to beat their *Tió de Nadal* (a smiling log) with sticks until it secretes presents. We kid you not.

HAVE A GRAPE YEAR

Come midnight, locals welcome the new year by stuffing a grape into their mouth with each strike of the clock.

CARNAVAL

Lent is a sober affair in Catalunya so locals make the most of Carnaval – the last hurrah before 40 days of fasting. The week-long party includes fancy dress competitions and parades galore, while Sitges *(p183)* hosts an adults-only version.

There's an art to being a Barcelonan, from the dos and don'ts on the beach to negotiating the city's streets. Here's a breakdown of all you need to know.

Barcelona
KNOW-HOW

For a directory of health and safety resources, safe spaces and accessibility information, turn to page 186. For everything else, read on.

EAT
Except for breakfast, which is munched on the hoof, eating is a social affair and never rushed in Barcelona. Lunch is the main meal of the day and eaten from 2pm, followed by a siesta. Dinners are lighter and kick off any time after 8pm. At the weekend, an aperitif is a must, as is the beloved post-dinner *sobretaula* – the tradition of chatting around the table, coffees and digestifs in hand.

DRINK
Pavement bars and cafés are second living rooms for Barcelonans, who often head down to their local to read the paper with a coffee or catch-up with a

friend. If you're sitting outside, the staff will come out to take your order; if you're inside, you'll generally be expected to order at the counter. These laid-back spots close around midnight, or an hour later on weekends.

SHOP
All the usual suspects (hello Zara) line the city's main shopping streets but locals prefer to shop in the city's indie stores and markets (where haggling is a no-no). Wherever you're spending your hard-earned cash, it's always worth carrying a tote bag to avoid the charge for a plastic one.

Shops open at 9am and close at 8 or 9pm, with smaller businesses shutting their doors between 2 and 4pm for lunch. On Sundays, pretty much everything closes for at least the afternoon, if not the whole day.

ARTS & CULTURE

Culture comes at a price in Barcelona, with many museums charging €10–13. The good news is a lot of places are free to enter at least one afternoon a week or month – check museum websites for details. Theatre, spoken word and comedy is largely performed in Catalan or Spanish. Fancy a gig instead? Barcelonans love live music, so it's wise to book any and all concerts in advance to avoid disappointment.

NIGHTLIFE

A chilled night out in Barna involves a few drinks with friends at a pavement bar or terrace. Those looking to go big, meanwhile, start with "pre-drinks" at home before hitting the clubs any time after 2am (an afternoon siesta is a must). Dancing continues until 5 or 6am, when the clubs shut, so many welcome the morning with a final drink at a dive bar or on the beach at sunrise. There's no need to dress up but beachwear and flip-flops will attract some eye-rolls.

OUTDOORS

Barcelonans are an outdoorsy bunch, whiling away their days in the park or on the beach. Off to join them on the sand? Keep a close eye on your belongings as pickpocketing is a problem. As for rubbish, there's loads of recycling bins across the city so be sure to do your bit (*guiris*, aka tourists, are known for being litterbugs, a reputation we want to help stamp out). Oh, and don't forget sunscreen.

Keep in mind

Here are some more tips and tidbits that will help you fit in like a local.

» **Cash vs card** The majority of places accept contactless payments but it's always worth keeping some cash on you.

» **No smoking** There's a ban on smoking inside and on a handful of city beaches. If you do need to light up, do so in a designated smoking area.

» **Tipping** It's polite to tip waiters and bar staff a few euros, but it's not obligatory.

» **Stay hydrated** Barna is home to countless free drinking fountains, so bring a resuable bottle to fill up on your travels.

GETTING AROUND

Catalunya's capital is divided into a handful of *barris*, or neighbourhoods *(p14)*, where some 1.6 million people live. Most of Barcelona is organized on a grid system, particularly the neighbourhoods of Eixample and Poblenou; with the Collserola mountains behind them and the gridded streets sloping down to the sea beyond, it's easy to get your bearings around these parts. The older winding streets of the Gothic Quarter and Raval are more confusing. Just remember: Las Ramblas runs straight between them from Plaça de Catalunya to the water's edge.

To help you out, we've provided what3words addresses for each sight in this book, meaning you can quickly pinpoint exactly where you're heading.

On foot

Barcelona is not a big city, so it's easy to get around on foot. Some steeper *barris* even have escalators to take the edge off. And, on weekends, the council closes off some of the main streets to traffic, allowing pedestrians more space and less fumes. Nice, eh? Of course, walking in the heat can be tiring. Be sure to have plenty of water and check out the Cool Walks website to plan your route through the city's most shaded streets.

Life in Barcelona is more slow-paced than in other European cities, so you won't have locals hot on your heels. That said, if you need to stop and check your phone or take a photo, step aside to let them sidle past.
https://cool.bcnregional.com

On wheels

Barcelonans love pedal power, with many locals choosing to cycle to work. Bike lanes generally follow the city's one-way system. The traffic light system also applies to bikes, so never go through a red light (even if you see fellow cyclists doing it). Cycling on the pavement when you could be in a bike lane will be met by shouts, and cycling with headphones is illegal – the police are strict about this. It's also illegal to cycle over the limit (0.5mg of alcohol per litre of blood, which works out as a pint of beer). Finally, always wear a helmet. No excuses.

The council's bike sharing scheme, Bicing, is only available for residents. Good news: Donkey Republic provides bikes that anyone can pick up and drop off around the city using its app. It's €3.50 for an hour, €5 for two hours or €10 for 24 hours. A lot of locals prefer to nip around the city on mopeds. For those who don't own their own, sharing

schemes from eCooltra and Yego are on hand to rent mopeds by the hour or day.
www.donkey.bike
www.cooltra.com
www.rideyego.com

By public transport

Barcelona's transport network, which is run by TMB, includes the metro, bus and tram. The metro runs from 5am to midnight on weekdays and until 2am on weekends (this is Barcelona, after all). While the metro map is easy enough to use, the bus map can seem daunting. Just remember: the H lines run horizontally, the V lines run vertically and the D lines diagonally. You've got this.

Download and register with TMB's app and use your smartphone as a contactless ticket. Prefer a good old paper ticket? Buy a "T-Casual" ticket for €11.35 and get ten trips across the network.

By car and taxi

Parking in Barna is no easy feat. This is largely intentional; the council is transforming traffic lanes into pavement space and bike lanes, much to the approval of eco-conscious locals. While many aren't, therefore, investing in cars, they are still taking taxis, preferring sharing services like Cabify (no Uber here), especially after a night out.

Download these

We recommend you download these apps to help you get about the city.

WHAT3WORDS
Your geocoding friend

A what3words address is a simple way to communicate any precise location on earth, using just three words. ///divides.sharp.desktop, for example, is the code for the entrance to the Gaudí House Museum. Simply download the free what3words app, type a what3words address into the search bar, and you'll know exactly where to go.

TMBAPP
Your local transit advice

The app from TMB, the Barcelona transport service, helps you plan your journey, find your nearest bus stop or station, check for operating hours and delays, and use your smartphone as a contactless ticket.

Each and every **barri** *(neighbourhood) in Barna has its own history and culture – and is very proud of the fact. Here we take a look at some of our favourites.*

Barcelona
NEIGHBOURHOODS

Barceloneta

Glitzy hotels and an artificial beach might tempt the tourists but this district also offers old-school bodegas and traditional street parties. Once a fishing village, Barceloneta became a refuge for families forced out of Born thanks to the construction of Parc de la Ciutadella in the 1800s. It's no wonder, then, that the *barri*'s locals – descendants of displaced families – actively protest against gentrification in their patch today. *{map 5}*

Born

Technically called "Sant Pere, Santa Catalina i la Ribera", Born is a labyrinth of medieval streets. Locals expertly navigate these alleyways, ducking into the *barri*'s artisan stores and workshops, just as locals did centuries ago. *{map 1}*

Eixample

Vast and gridded Eixample buzzes with life, day and night. Through the *barri*'s heart runs Passeig de Gràcia, a grand old street lined with *Modernista* mansions, high-end stores and swanky restaurants. Either side of this thoroughfare is where middle-class families go about their days, picking the kids up from school and swinging by their local library. Around the quadrants of Universitat, LGBTQ+ folk and their allies live their best lives in "Gaixample"'s rip-roaring bars. *{map 4}*

Gothic Quarter

Neighbourhoods don't come more historical than this place. Roman ruins, ancient streets and a medieval Jewish quarter attract throngs of wide-eyed tourists. As for the locals? They prefer the Gothic Quarter's shabby-chic bars, hidden down the streets toward the sea. *{map 1}*

Gràcia

Once a town on the outskirts of the city, Gràcia is nirvana for young families who can't get enough of the bohemian *barri*'s organic shops, vermouth bars and vegan cafés. Locals live life publicly here, spending lazy mornings and sociable afternoons in the pavement cafés that circle the neighbourhood's squares. {map 4}

Montjuïc

Ah, Montjuïc: the stunning setting of the 1992 Olympic Games. Sure, it's more of a string of parks than a traditional neighbourhood, but Barna's Magic Mountain teems with life nonetheless. Families hold outdoor celebrations in its green spaces, folks enjoy a dose of culture at its world-class museums and wannabe Olympians make use of the running tracks. {map 3}

Poblenou

The former hub of Barcelona's industry is now the heartland of young coffee-clutching professionals. Old factories house artists' studios and cultural centres, plus the tech sector "Districte 22". Barcelona's version of Silicon Valley, this urban renewal project is aimed at tech start-ups. {map 5}

Poble Sec

Multicultural and working-class Poble Sec has managed to keep its edge in a city that's fast-gentrifying. The little barri, at the foot of Montjuïc, is hard to beat for top-quality tapas joints, cheap and cheerful dive bars, and lively nightclubs. {map 3}

Raval

Mischief has long been the hallmark of this notorious part of town. Once a hot bed of crime and sex work, the barri has since seen an influx of immigration, with families from Latin America, the Philippines and Pakistan settling here. Kebab shops and falafel stands buzz with energy in the evening, when good-timers stop to refuel on wild nights out in the city's most rebellious neighbourhood. {map 2}

Sant Antoni

Hot on Gràcia's heels as a hipster's paradise is Sant Antoni. The uber-cool barri is awash with bougie brunch spots and trendy clothing stores, plus old-school Catalan restaurants and charming orxateries. {map 3}

Sants

A working-class district to its core, Sants stands firm as the final frontier against gentrification. Cultural associations, workers' cooperatives and traditional businesses form the social fabric of this residential outpost. {map 6}

Sarrià

The upper parts of the city (in and around the rolling Collserola hills) are also home to its upper classes. Sarrià is one such posh patch. Expect beautiful townhouses, expensive wine bars and fancy gourmet shops galore. {map 6}

Tibidabo and Vallvidrera

Only rich folk – those even richer than Sarrià residents – can afford to live in these leafy neighbourhoods, set up high in the Collserola hills. For those who can only dream, the surroundings are perfect for gusty weekend hikes and scenic bike rides. {map 6}

Barcelona
ON THE MAP

Whether you're looking for your new favourite spot or want to check out what each part of Barcelona has to offer, our maps – along with handy map references throughout the book – have you covered.

Parc de Collserol

TIBIDABO

RONDA DE DAI

SARRIÀ

AVINGUDA

B23

A2

SANT FELIU DE LLOBREGAT

ESPLUGUES DE LLOBREGAT

CARRER D

B23

CORNELLÀ DE LLOBREGAT

L'HOSPITALET DE LLOBREGAT

A2

El Llobregat

SANT BOI DE LLOBREGAT

C31

PLAÇA
D'URQUINAONA

C. DE TRAFALGAR

SANT PERE

Plaça de Sant **O**
Agustí Vell

A Palau de la Música
Catalana

Antic Teatre **N**

E Le Cucine
Mandarosso

S Humana Vintage

S Raima

S Mercat de Santa
Caterina

D Planelles Donat

La Casa del **A**
Entremesos

E Bar del Pla

Marlowe Bar

A Els Quatre Gats

PLAÇA
D'ANTONI
MAURA

BORN

Museu Picasso **A**

Can Cisa **D**   Moco Museum **A**

La
Chinata

PLAÇA
NOVA

Bodega la Puntual **E**

GOTHIC
QUARTER

Dr Stravinsky **D**   Estimar **E**
Angle Store **S**

PLAÇA
DE L'ANGEL

Bon Vent **S**

E El Chigre 1

Xocolates **S**
Fargas

The Espadrilles
Experience

Cafés el **D**
Magnífico

La Botifarreria
de Santa Mari

Taller de **A**
4 Pintors

La Nostra
Ciutat **S**

Plaça de **O**
Sant Felip Neri

Conesa **E**

S Casa Carot

L'Arca **S**

E La Alcoba Azul
D Zona d'Ombra

Dulcinea **D**

MUHBA
El Call **A**

PLAÇA DE
SANT JAUME

Collage **D**
S Vila Vinite
"La Teca"

Ganiveteria **S O**
Roca   Plaça
del Pi

PLAÇA
D'ANTONI
LOPEZ

PLAÇA DELS
TRAGINERS

CARRER DE LA BOQUERIA

E Can Culleretes

S Llibreria Cómplices

PORT VELL

PLAÇA
DE LA
BOQUERIA

N Sidecar

CARRER   D'AVINYO

Manchester **N**

PLAÇA
REIAL

N Marula
Café

Jamboree **N**
Jazz

N Ocaña

Polaroid
Bar **N**

PLAÇA DE
LA MERCE

N
Macarena
Club

0 metres   250

0 yards   250

PLAÇA DEL DUC
DE MEDINACELI

MAP 1

Parc de la
Ciutadella

1

PASSEIG DE PICASSO

E
San Pedrito

El Born Centre
de Cultura
A i Memòria

PLAÇA COMERCIAL

N
Guzzo Club

AV. DEL MARQUÈS
DE L'ARGENTERA

D Bar Paradiso

PLAÇA DEL
PALAU

RONDA LITORAL

E EAT

Bar del Pla *(p48)*
Bodega la Puntual *(p51)*
Can Culleretes *(p33)*
Conesa *(p46)*
El Chigre 1769 *(p39)*
Estimar *(p55)*
La Alcoba Azul *(p49)*
Le Cucine Mandarosso *(p52)*
San Pedrito *(p52)*

D DRINK

Bar Paradiso *(p79)*
Cafés el Magnífico *(p69)*
Can Cisa *(p67)*
Collage *(p78)*
Dr Stravinsky *(p78)*
Dulcinea *(p80)*
Marlowe Bar *(p76)*
Planelles Donat *(p82)*
Zona d'Ombra *(p65)*

S SHOP

Angle Store *(p104)*
Bon Vent *(p96)*
Casa Carot *(p111)*
Ganiveteria Roca *(p99)*
Humana Vintage *(p88)*
La Botifarreria de Santa Maria
(p110)
La Chinata *(p110)*
La Nostra Ciutat *(p98)*
L'Arca *(p89)*

Llibreria Cómplices *(p95)*
Mercat de Santa Caterina *(p109)*
Raima *(p96)*
Vila Viniteca "La Teca" *(p108)*
Xocolates Fargas *(p110)*

A ARTS & CULTURE

El Born Centre de Cultura i
Memòria *(p118)*
Els Quatre Gats *(p120)*
The Espadrilles Experience *(p134)*
La Casa del Entremesos *(p128)*
Moco Museum *(p126)*
MUHBA El Call *(p118)*
Museu Picasso *(p124)*
Palau de la Música Catalana *(p121)*
Taller de 4 Pintors *(p133)*

N NIGHTLIFE

Antic Teatre *(p156)*
Guzzo Club *(p150)*
Jamboree Jazz *(p155)*
Macarena Club *(p147)*
Manchester *(p151)*
Marula Café *(p146)*
Ocaña *(p149)*
Polaroid Bar *(p150)*
Sidecar *(p146)*

O OUTDOORS

Plaça del Pi *(p171)*
Plaça de Sant Augustí Vell *(p171)*
Plaça de Sant Felip Neri *(p170)*

MAP 2

2

PLAÇA
NOVA

GOTHIC
QUARTER

PLAÇA
DE SANT
JAUME

CARRER DE FERRAN

PLAÇA
REIAL

LA RAMBLA

Moog

Bar Pastís

Cangrejo

Arts Santa
Mònica

RASSANES

PLAÇA DE LES
DRASSANES

MAP 3

Las Vermudas **D**

Bar Salvatge **D**

E Veg World India

Rabipelao **E**
N Heliogàbal

La Ceba **E** Xocolateria
La Nena **S** Entre Latas
Atuell Ceràmica **A** **D**
D Bodega
Hibernian **S** Art&Wine **A** E. Marín
Plaça del Sol **O** CARRER DE BAILEN

D Syra

GRÀCIA

El Genio **S** **D** Bar Raim
Equivocado

La Vermu **D** **O**
Ladyloquita **S** Plaça de la **S** Casa Atlântica **E** Ramen-Ya
Vila de Gràcia Hiro

Bar Bodega **D**
Quimet **D** Lo Pinyol

D Slow Mov

E Entrepanes
Díaz

E Berbena

Fat **E**
Veggies **E** **S** La Central
Bar Torpedo

A Casa
Fundació **A** Amatller
Tàpies
Silan Cotton
Besta **E** Vintage
S **E** **E** **N** Carita Bonita
Jazz Curtis **N**
Messengers Audiophile Café Robata
N Believe
Club **S** Finestres

E La Bikineria
S Altaïr

D Senyor Vermut La Chapelle **N**
Mont Bar **E**
E Cameua
Candy Darling **N**

EIXAMPLE

PLAÇA DE LA
UNIVERSITAT

RAVAL

0 metres   400
0 yards   400

MAP 4

4

CÓRSEGA

DIAGONAL

A Quadrat d'Or

CATALANES

PLAÇA D'URQUINAONA

PLAÇA DE CATALUNYA

A Barcelona Civil War Tour

GOTHIC QUARTER

LA RAMBLA

A Disseny Hub

Ceramic Art
Studio 137º **A**

D Balius

Barcelon
Beach Hous

D El Tío Che

PLAÇA DE
LES GLÒRIES

Espai
Joliu **D**

S Ultra-Local
Records

N L'Auditori

POBLENOU **A** IDEAL

EIXAMPLE

N Razzmatazz

N Càmping

E Roots & Rolls

E Funky Bakers Deli

S Pitagora

D Bodega
Bonay

Satan's Coffee **D** **D**
Corner

A Biblioteca Publica Arús

News & Coffee

SANT MARTÍ

BLAW Store **S**

Platja
Nova Icària

Kanay Taller **A**
de Ceràmica

Nomad
Coffee Lab **D**

S Inèrcia Rollerblade
Rental

S Petit Encants

Flax & Kale **E**

S **D** Bodega
Maestrazgo

O

Port
Olímpic

Barcelona
City Records

Parc de la
Ciutadella

PLAÇA DE
CATALUNYA

Zoo de
Barcelona

PLAÇA
NOVA

BORN

Platja
Somorrostro

GOTHIC
QUARTER

Bar Jai-Ca **E** **E** Cheriff

RAVAL

O Espigó del Gas

Compá **E**

D Bar Leo

Platja
Barceloneta

BARCELONETA

PORT
VELL

O Ungravity SUP & Surf

PLAÇA DEL
PORTAL
DE LA PAU

PLAÇA
DEL MAR

Platja de
Sant Miquel

POBLE SEC

Mediterranean
Sea

Platja de
Sant Sebastià

0 metres   750

0 yards   750

O Plaça de la Rosa dels Vents

MAP 5

5

Skatepark
Mar Bella
⊙

*Platja de
la Mar Bella*

*atja del
ogatell*

Parc de
Collserola

Parc del
Laberint d'Horta **O**

RONDA DE DALT

AVINGUDA MERIDIANA

RONDA LLIC

HORTA

SANT ANDREU
DE PALOMAR

Barcelona Wood
A Workshops

TIBIDABO

Parc
Güell

MUHBA Turó
O de la Rovira

SANT
MARTÍ

Gaudí House
Museum **A**

Hospital de la
A Santa Creu i Sant Pau

GRAN VIA DE LES CORTS CATALA

Bellesguard **A**

Bodega
Manolo **D**

AVINGUDA

RONDA DE DALT

Mantequerías
Pirenaicas **E**

GRÀCIA

POBLENOU

DIAGONAL

On y va **D**

AVINGUDA

DIAGONAL

A Monestir de
Pedralbes

Avec Studio **S**

EIXAMPLE

See maps 1–5 for
Central Barcelona

SARRIÀ

DIAGONAL

AVINGUDA

GOTHIC
QUARTER

D Trencalòs

CARRER DE LES CORTS CATALANES

RAVAL

BARCELONETA

Parc de l'Espanya Industrial **O**

CARRER DE SANTS

Petit Pau **E**

SANTS

GRAN VIA DE LES CORTS CATALANES

MONTJUÏC

CARRER DE SANTA EULÀLIA

Mediterranean
Sea

0 kilometres   1

0 miles   1

MAP 6

E EAT

D DRINK

S SHOP

A ARTS & CULTURE

N NIGHTLIFE

O OUTDOORS

EAT

Feasts whipped up by families, plates of tasty tapas passed between loved ones, creative dishes crafted by plucky chefs: eating out in Barna is all about celebrating life.

Traditional Fare

Catalans are fiercely – and rightly – proud of their cuisine. Barcelona has loads of traditional (read: old-school) spots plating up classic Catalan and Spanish dishes. Here is a taster to whet your appetite.

PETIT PAU

Map 6; Carrer de l'Espanya Industrial, 22, Sants;
///slower.sprayed.milk; www.petitpau.cat

Petit, as you may have guessed, is Catalan for "small", and that's the perfect word to describe this rustic restaurant, which has space for just 16 lucky diners. The menu is equally compact, though there are veggie, vegan and gluten-free options for those in want. Owner Pau is there to talk you through his takes on classic Catalan dishes

Try it!
COOK LIKE A CATALAN

Looking to learn from the masters? Born to Cook offers various gourmet experiences. Better yet, the class leaders will help you navigate Barcelona's vast Santa Caterina market *(www.borntocookbarcelona.com)*.

and flavours. Intrigued to know how the turbot with turnips is prepared? Want to hear more about the roasted goat with liquorice sauce? Pau will happily explain all.

L'ESTUPENDU

Map 6; Carrer d'Eduard Maristany, 75, Badalona;
///scooped.jumped.bake; www.grupovarela.es/l-estupendu

Step in past the palm trees and blue picket fence and take a seat under the shade of the straw roof at L'Estupendu. Being by the seafront, seafood is, of course, king at this beach restaurant, so a paella-style rice dish is a lunchtime must, and the perfect thing to share with friends while gazing out to sea.

» Don't leave without sharing an *arròs del fadrí*, a seafood rice dish in which all the seafood comes mercifully ready peeled.

CAN CULLERETES

Map 1; Carrer d'en Quintana, 5, Gothic Quarter;
///exacted.beeline.sizes; www.culleretes.com

With wrought-iron chandeliers and elaborate wall tapestries, Can Culleretes oozes all the character you'd expect to find in Catalunya's oldest restaurant (it was founded way back when in 1796). The menu likewise has all the essential pickings of Catalan cuisine: meatballs with cuttlefish, stuffed aubergines, *botifarra* sausages. But don't go thinking all that history and top-notch grub comes with a hefty price tag; the set lunch menu is a steal. *Bon profit!* (That's *bon appétit* in Catalan.)

CAMEUA

Map 4; Carrer de Mallorca, 77, Eixample; ///recent.convert.tedious;
640 605 405

Cosy Cameua is all about making diners nostalgic for home-style food, just like their mamas made. Join friends swapping stories over traditional foods from across the peninsula, like croquettes and cod fritters. Round off your meal with the Catalan tradition of *sobretaula* by ordering a digestif and chatting long after you've finished eating.

NA MINDONA

Map 2; Carrer de la Riereta, 8; ///terminology.burst.spending;
www.namindona.es

You could easily walk past Na Mindona were it not for the vase of flowers that Xisca – one of the friendliest restaurateurs in town – sets outside every day. Watch her flit between tables and chat to her guests like old friends, talking them through her Majorcan menu. Our favourite dish? It's between the fishy rice stew and tongue with capers.

» Don't leave without finishing with a digestif of the traditional Majorcan *licor d'herbes*. *Salut!*

CAN VILARÓ

Map 3; Carrer del Comte Borrell, 61, Sant Antoni;
///budget.cashew.leans; 933 250 578

For three generations the Vilaró family have been keeping the working people of Sant Antoni well fed. Even while much of the *barri* (neighbourhood) has gentrified and succumbed to food fads, the Vilaró family has stayed true to traditional Catalan cuisine in its meatiest forms (pig trotters, lamb lungs and blood sausage all feature heavily on the menu). Rest easy: there are dishes for the more faint-hearted, but when in Barcelona…

LA CEBA

Map 4; Carrer de la Perla, 10, Gràcia; ///hills.overnight.elastic; www.lacebabcn.com

Anyone familiar with Spanish cuisine will be aware of the humble *tortilla de patatas* (a traditional Spanish omelette bulked out with potatoes). La Ceba takes this classic dish to a whole new level with some 50 types of omelette, each served with a slice of mouth-wateringly good tomato-drenched toast (a Catalan staple). It's these endless varieties of omelettes – and the good-value set-menu lunches – that keep Gràcia locals coming back.

Yes, Les Ramblas is a tourist trap. But behind the souvenir stores and pricey pavement cafés hides the odd treasure, like Louro *(Rambla de los Capuchinos, 37)*. Few seem to have cottoned on to the fact that this charming Galician restaurant is tucked away on the first floor of an old palace. Enter under the Hostal Benidorm sign and climb the stairs up to Louro, where couples chow down on Galician-style octopus and smugly toast to their choice of restaurant.

Creative Cuisine

Classic fare will always have its place but Barcelona is also a city of innovation and reinvention. Not all these creative spots are uber-fancy, but all of them promise unadulterated deliciousness.

BODEGA BONAY

Map 5; Gran Via de les Corts Catalanes, 700, Eixample;
///luck.robots.ensemble; www.casabonay.com

Found within the hip Casa Bonay hotel, Bodega Bonay curates small plates of mostly Catalan influence, with ingredients heavily dependent on the season. Our top tip? Come here in winter. The stuff they do with sea urchins is magic, and the cavatelli pasta with lamb ragout is the ultimate bowl of comfort. Round off your meal at the rooftop bar.

CRUIX

Map 3; Carrer d'Entença, 57, Eixample; ///woods.rebounds.dampen;
www.cruixrestaurant.com

Valencian chef Miquel Pardo cooked all around Spain before opening Cruix in Eixample. It's here that locals book a table when they want to splash out on a swanky meal without blowing their entire month's salary. The very reasonable tasting menu is lined with fusion dishes, like hake churros with a salsa verde and Pardo's signature *fuet nigiri* (a Catalan salami). And, good news: Pardo stays true to his roots by including an excellent rice course (we'd expect nothing less from a chef hailing from the home of paella).

DOS PEBROTS

Map 2; Carrer del Dr Dou, 19, Raval; ///stubbed.sedated.racing; www.dospebrots.com

Embark on a voyage through time with chef Albert Raurich, who is quite the culinary historian. Each item on his menu is rooted in a point in Mediterranean history and reimagined to give it 21st-century flair (Raurich studied numerous books for research). Take the open-faced Roman omelette, prepared tableside with pine nuts and anchovy garum. The menu lists each dish's background so you and your pals will know precisely which decade you're chomping your way through.

>> Don't leave without trying the Persian kebab (1,500 BC), which you'll assemble yourself. Slow-cooked lamb and fresh pitta bread – joyous.

MONT BAR

Map 4; Carrer de la Diputació, 220, Eixample; ///info.limes.cotton; www.montbar.com

A lip-smacking selection of regional wines is paired with fresh takes on Catalan cuisine at this upscale bistro-style restaurant. Yes, these dishes are local at heart but prepared with a clear French pedigree and enhanced with international flavours; think cucumber carbonara, Cantonese suckling pig and cockle soufflé.

BERBENA

Map 4; Carrer de Minerva, 6, Gràcia; ///vibrate.dragging.puddle;
www.berbenabcn.com

Having worked in Michelin-star kitchens at home and abroad, local
boy Carlos Pérez de Rozas left the world of fine dining and made his
way back to Barna to do things on his own terms. Using seasonal
ingredients, he reimagines Catalan classics, creating a menu that
changes often. Check out the socials of local foodies, who regularly
update their feeds with Berbena's latest offerings, for a sneak preview.

SUCULENT

Map 2; Rambla del Raval, 45, Raval; ///spoon.contacts.gather;
www.suculent.com

Best described as the lovechild of a French brasserie and Catalan
grandma's kitchen, Suculent sits tucked away at the bottom of the
Rambla del Raval. Here you'll find local chefs checking out the
competition and hungry lunch-goers chatting loudly over one another,
all keen to show their appreciation of the nose-to-tail cuisine.

BESTA

Map 4; Carrer d'Aribau, 106, Eixample; ///shorts.prelude.future;
www.bestabarcelona.com

Why limit your cooking to only one region when Spain's bounty
stretches from coast to coast? This was the thinking of chefs Manu
Núñez and Carles Ramon, the former from northwestern Galicia
and the latter from here in Catalunya. Besta is a celebration of the

two regions' cuisines, marrying the flavours of the Atlantic and the Mediterranean. The menu changes so often that if you come again you'll likely be greeted with something entirely different to tuck into.

TABERNA NOROESTE

Map 3; Carrer de Radas, 67, Poble Sec; ///zooms.troubled.boat; www.tabernanoroeste.com

Fire-roasted peppers with San Simón cheese and Cantabrian anchovies, Castilian-style suckling lamb with Galician potatoes: it's all about the flavours of the north and west of Spain at this ultra-hip spot. Scenesters know to ask for a table by the open kitchen where they can watch the chefs expertly prepare creative small plates.

EL CHIGRE 1769

Map 1; Carrer dels Sombrerers, 7, Born; ///probing.husbands.investor; www.elchigre1769.com

Nestled behind the medieval church of Santa Maria del Mar, in an 18th-century stone building, El Chigre is a glow-up of a traditional Asturian cider tavern. Yes, there are the ubiquitous heaps of fresh seafood on ice and bunches of garlic hanging from rustic ceiling beams. The dishes, though, are wholly refined; downsized and carefully crafted, creative plates include octopus doused with seaweed "chimichurri" sauce and prawns served on a bed of black rice.

» Don't leave without trying the Asturian cider, a very tart and non-carbonated drink that requires a specific pouring technique. Ask your server for a demo, or simply follow your neighbour's lead.

Veggie and Vegan

*Long gone are the days when Barcelonan cooks
slipped chunks of ham or chorizo into almost
every dish. Today the city is a veritable cornucopia
of meat-free offerings.*

VEG WORLD INDIA

Map 4; Carrer de Bruniquer, 24, Gràcia; ///ruffle.kinks.turned;
www.vegworldindiabarcelona.es

Gràcia locals jostle at the tables of this popular spot, tucking into
steaming baskets of fresh naan (there are nine varieties), spicy bowls of
chickpea chana masala and delicate paneer dosa. Most dishes on the
100 per cent vegetarian menu can be made vegan too (just ask). Opt
for the "Indian Specialities" section of the menu for hearty helpings
of aloo gobi (potato and cauliflower curry) and bhindi baji okra.

RABIPELAO

Map 4; Carrer del Torrent d'En Vidalet 22, Gràcia; ///skipped.foal.flicks;
www.elrabipelao.com

Sometimes the strangest combinations work the best. Take
Rabipelao: a dining room decked out like a British neo-Victorian
cabaret that plates up veggie and vegan takes on Venezuelan

classics, like *arepas* (stuffed cornmeal patties) and *tequeños* (cheese-filled fried breadsticks). Treating a friend for their birthday? Order the sharing platter and prepare to gorge yourselves on every dish on the menu.

» **Don't leave without** rounding off your feast of a meal with a flaming mai tai out on Rabipelao's shabby-chic patio.

FLAX & KALE
Map 5; Carrer de Sant Pere Més Alt, 31, 33, Sant Pere;
///minerals.invented.shady; www.flaxandkale.com

Brainchild of Catalan chef and plant-based pioneer Teresa Carles, Flax & Kale is technically flexitarian so you'll see a smattering of dairy, eggs and fish on the menu. Glaze over this and instead head straight for the list of wood-fired pizzas, which are entirely vegan, gluten-free and, quite frankly, to die for (even if you're a total cheese fiend). Try the vegan truffle pizza with coconut cream, wild mushrooms and truffle oil – trust us, it's sublime.

Hidden away between Raval and Sant Antoni, hole-in-the-wall bar Jonny Aldana serves up Latin American vegan fast food *(www.jonnyaldana.com)*. Clubbers call in at the night-time-only bar to fuel up on meat-free nachos and tacos. When a DJ appears (usually at weekends), the night's plans are inevitably forgotten – why move on?

Liked by the locals

"Arriving in the 2000s, the best a vegan could expect was a stare of incomprehension. Now the scene is completely different. Many restaurants offer dishes like fermented black bean salsa brava, tempeh chicken burgers, veggie fast food and vegan jackfruit tacos."

BÉATRIX LUJUA, FOOD WRITER AND CHEF

CACTUS CAT BAR

Map 2; Carrer de Valldonzella 52, Raval; ///snoring.showcase.civil; www.cactusbar.cat

Owners Carlos and Gilbert are generous with everything at Cactus Cat Bar; you'll be met with their big smiles and even bigger portions. Everything here, from the burgers to the *croquetas*, is 100 per cent vegan and 100 per cent homemade. You won't want to leave.

ROOTS & ROLLS

Map 5; Carrer del Consell de Cent, 401, Eixample; ///appear.changes.shades; www.rootsandrolls.com

Uber-stylish Roots & Rolls is the go-to place for a working lunch. Chew over that latest project while enjoying vegan Japanese comfort foods such as gyoza and *okonomiyaki* (savoury pancakes), or perhaps some plant-based sushi.

» **Don't leave without** sampling "Heura", the soya-based chicken substitute that was invented right here in Barcelona.

FAT VEGGIES

Map 4; Carrer de París, 168, Eixample; ///nowadays.lazy.hotels; www.fatveggies.com

You'll be transported to the barbecue joints of the American South at Fat Veggies, a self-proclaimed "vegetarian smokehouse" where organic veg gets seared, smoked and charred. Don't be mistaken though: the influences and flavours are entirely Mediterranean (think roasted carrots doused in a tomato-rich *romesco* sauce).

Cheap Eats

*When it comes to cheap and cheerful bites, Barna
delivers. Locals graze on sandwiches for elevenses
(brunch isn't a thing here), gobble quick lunches and
gorge on gourmet burgers before a night of partying.*

BAR TORPEDO

Map 4; Carrer d'Aribau, 143, local 1, Eixample;
///responds.bunks.oatmeal; www.bartorpedo.com

The vibe at Bar Torpedo is part retro NYC diner, part highbrow wine
bar thanks to the mix of double patty melt burgers and natural
wines. Here diners devour their soft-shell crab and beef tongue
pastrami burgers with greasy fingers, pausing to swill curious wines
from around Catalunya. With burgers costing €8 or so, this is the
perfect place for a meal when a bit of affordable indulgence is in order.

RAMEN-YA HIRO

Map 4; Carrer de Girona 164, Gràcia; ///speaking.pleasing.tides;
930 028 441

People never queue for a restaurant in Barcelona (life's way too
short), unless that restaurant is Ya Hiro. And what are they waiting
for? Chef Hiroki Yoshiyuki's sublime ramen, that's what. Hiroki

If you're too hungry to queue, but still fancy Japanese food, try Yoi Yoi Gion, just a few minutes away.

spent years fine-tuning the recipe and watches over the pot of bubbling broth for hours each day. With patience comes pure perfection.

FUNKY BAKERS DELI

Map 5; Carrer de la Diputació, 347, Eixample; ///shields.supply.quirky; www.funkybakers.com

What began as a small bakery and take-away window on the Passeig del Born has grown, thanks to huge demand, into this second, larger bakery and café. Founder Seyma's Turkish roots are merged with food traditions from around Europe; braided challah bread and cardamom babkas share menu space with Danish-style smørrebrød and wickedly creamy Basque cheesecake.

» Don't leave without sampling the *borek*, a savoury, slightly spicy Turkish pastry of coiled filo dough stuffed with potatoes and herbs.

MANTEQUERÍAS PIRENAICAS

Map 6; Carrer de Muntaner, 460, Sarrià-Sant Gervasi; ///hours.liberty.declares; 932 019 189

Remember: Spaniards eat lunch around 2pm, after which it's siesta time. Too peckish to wait until then? Head to this cheery little spot around noon for an *aperitiu* (small bite before a meal) before the staff snap the doors shut and mosey on home for a bite to eat and a snooze. A *canya* (small beer), *flauta* (mini sandwich) and olives to share amid the loud chatter will make you feel like a true Barcelonan.

LA BIKINERIA

Map 4; Carrer de Mallorca, 135, Eixample; ///dots.risen.monument;
www.labikineria.es

Here in Barcelona, a *bikini* isn't just a piece of swimwear, it's also a cheese-and-ham toastie. This staple snack is found at almost every bar and café but La Bikineria is the one place that takes the humble *bikini* to a whole new level, using gourmet ingredients from the Ninot Market. We're talking things like black sausage and oozy brie.

FALAFEL OF SHANI

Map 2; La Rambla, 91, Mercat de la Boqueria, 133–134, Raval;
///unites.tweeted.cotton; www.falafelboqueria.com

La Boqueria market *(p109)* has loads of restaurants that serve up the bounty of the city, but that bounty is rarely vegan. Enter Falafel of Shani, the handiwork of Israeli cook Shani Waytzman. Expect hot and fluffy pitta stuffed with fresh falafel (Shani learned the recipe from her father), your choice of toppings (thin slices of fried aubergine are our favourite), and lashings of tahini and chilli oil. Gluten-free and kosher options are also available.

CONESA

Map 1; Carrer de la Llibreteria, 1, Gothic Quarter;
///routines.fires.emblem; www.conesaentrepans.com

The bustling square that houses the City Council and Catalan government has been home to another crucial institution for the last 60 years: Conesa. Barcelona's oldest sandwich joint continues to bring in droves of partygoers, all looking to line their stomachs with hearty baguettes before going big on nights out. Vegans and coeliacs, have no fear: there's a number of offerings for you too.

» Don't leave without grabbing one of the filled wasabi bread baguettes and finding a spot on Plaça Sant Miquel to eat it.

COMPÁ

Map 5; Carrer de Sant Carles, 19, Barceloneta; ///shark.unwell.branch; 623 312 282

After a morning sunning themselves on Barceloneta's beaches, bronzed locals have one place in mind: the tiny deli counter of Compá. Here Vittorio Cicero does his homeland of Calabria proud, whipping up paninis laden with juicy pork meatballs, spicy nduja sausage, long-simmered tomato sauce and loads of molten cheese. Panini devoured, it's straight back to the beach to bask in a food coma.

ENTREPANES DÍAZ

Map 4; Carrer de Pau Claris, 189, Eixample; ///tenses.market.bluffs; 934 157 582

When millennials want to show their parents that they've got their lives together, they make for Entrepanes Díaz. Mimicking a 1950s restaurant, the swanky sandwich shop serves up affordable gourmet lunches on vintage tableware. The owners make a point of hiring their friendly suited waiters over the age of 50 to keep up the charm of a classic spot while also providing jobs in what can be a cut-throat industry. What's not to love?

Tapear

"Tapear", or "to go for tapas", is key to city life. Unlike elsewhere in Spain, you won't get free tapas with your drink in Barcelona. Locals instead pay for the privilege to enjoy these tasty morsels.

BAR DEL PLA
Map 1; Carrer de Montcada, 2, Born; ///lavender.ally.pockets; www.bardelpla.cat

Tapas is given a dose of nostalgia at Bar del Pla, where seasonal specials are paired with what the staff lovingly call *plats de la iaia* (grandma dishes). These old-school Catalan dishes include beef cheeks in red wine, smoked sardine flatbreads and pig trotters.

BAR ALEGRÍA
Map 3; Carrer del Comte Borrell, 133, Sant Antoni; ///weds.pickles.shirt; 672 376 168

"Alegría" means joy and the staff at this lively *Modernista* bar certainly do the name justice. You'll likely hear your waiter bellow at the bar, asking for your *canya* (small glass of beer), to be met by smart retorts. On the food front, expect tapas with a twist. Written on a blackboard, the 15 or so dishes use top-quality ingredients and you'll see just how exceptionally well these are put to use after your first bite. If you're lucky, a bunch of musicians will show up to entertain the crowd in true Alegría style. Like we said: pure joy.

BAR JAI-CA

Map 5; Carrer de Ginebra, 13, Barceloneta; ///slab.pony.weeded; www.barjaica.com

Welcome to one of Barceloneta's classics, a bar that was once so raucous it landed the owner with an 18-month prison sentence for noise pollution. Things have calmed down a bit since then, but Bar Jai-Ca still has one of the liveliest atmospheres in the city, thanks to its regular crowd of tipsy good-timers and bronzed beachgoers, all chowing down on succulent seafood tapas.

LA ALCOBA AZUL

Map 1; Carrer de Salomó ben Adret, 14, Gothic Quarter; ///exposing.pints.tweaked; www.laalcobaazul.com

The tight, winding streets of Barcelona's old Jewish Quarter have an otherworldly magic about them. Nowhere epitomizes this more than La Alcoba Azul, a candlelit cave hidden in the heart of the *barri*. Couples cosy up at rickety tables, talking in hushed whispers as jazz music plays softly in the background. They're here for the bar's irresistible experimental tapas, like cod carpaccio and spiced baked tomatoes, which they pair with the bar's potent cocktails.

» Don't leave without sharing a classic Catalan dinner of *torrades* – large slices of toast piled high with a range of different treats.

Solo, Pair, Crowd

Whether you're meeting new people, on a date or making merry with the gang, *tapear* is all about socializing.

FLYING SOLO
Mingle with the locals

Sant Antoni's Bodega d'en Rafael is as local as it gets. Staff will ask you to tick what you want from a list of tapas before they go back to bantering with the regulars. Sit back and drink it all in.

IN A PAIR
Swanky tapas for two

Date on the horizon? Make a beeline for Viblioteca in Gràcia. A play on *vino* (wine) and *biblioteca* (library), Viblioteca does exactly what it says on the tin (or, er, bottle). Pluck a bottle from the shelves and enjoy with some seriously refined tapas.

FOR A CROWD
Get the party started

Your elbow will touch your neighbour's at buzzy La Bicicleta (you and your pals will likely make a whole new posse of friends). Fab vibes aside, this favourite spot promises classic Catalan tapas at reasonable prices.

BODEGA LA PUNTUAL

**Map 1; Carrer de Montcada, 22, Born; ///unstable.tune.gathers;
933 103 545**

This bodega was made for family gatherings. Expect to find big groups here: siblings laughing over glasses of vermouth, their kids greedily tucking into classic tapas and the grandparents inspecting the displays of cured meats and cheeses. Jolly and relaxed, this is what *tapeo* is all about.

BANYS VERGE DEL CARME

**Map 6; Carrer del Mar, 4B, Montgat; ///expires.headed.folders;
www.banysvergedelcarme.com**

Nothing beats eating tapas by the sea, the wind in your hair. Standing among the bathing huts on Montgat beach, this summertime shack is the perfect place for just that. Enjoy a beer and some seafood tapas before dipping your toe in the sea.

» Don't leave without trying the *cazón en adobo*, marinated and deep-fried dogfish (you won't want to share).

BODEGA AMPOSTA

**Map 3; Carrer d'Amposta, 1, Sants; ///gravest.author.resemble;
www.bodegaamposta.com**

With old wooden beams and polished marble surfaces, this outpost has all the reassuring trappings of a traditional tapas bar. But old-school, it is not. Brothers and owners Jordi and Josep give classic tapas a haute-cuisine flourish. The tasting menu is a great place to start.

Special Occasion

Entering a new decade? Secured that promotion? Put a ring on it? Barcelona might be a casual city but it's got a glut of restaurants that promise the glamour and gravitas that your big day deserves.

SAN PEDRITO

**Map 1; Carrer de la Fusina, 6, Born; ///recent.disputes.national;
www.sanpedritobcn.com**

Sometimes a celebration calls for tacos and, thankfully, Mexican joint San Pedrito is there for those moments. Moody lighting, fiery salsas and plenty of top-shelf mezcal make for the perfect jubilant meal. Clink glasses of smoky *espadín* with friends on the outdoor terrace, or enjoy a romantic one-on-one meal in the cosy dining room. Whatever the occasion, San Pedrito promises a fiesta.

LE CUCINE MANDAROSSO

**Map 1; Carrer de Verdaguer i Callís 4, Born; ///slicer.monkeys.curve;
www.lecucinemandarosso.com**

Walls stocked with gourmet ingredients, menus written up on blackboards and families chatting animatedly: Le Cucine Mandarosso has all the hallmarks of a picture-postcard Italian restaurant. As for the food, rest assured it's the full trattoria fantasy with recipes sourced from the owner's inner circle of Italian *nonnas*. Night-time is best for a relaxed à la carte meal with your nearest and dearest (the very reasonable set-menu lunch can make the place a little frantic).

» **Don't leave without** strolling round the corner to peruse the restaurant's emporium, stocked with all the finest goods from Italy.

CHERIFF

Map 5; Carrer de Ginebra, 15, Barceloneta; ///massive.bind.shots; www.cheriffrestaurant.es

Don't be put off by the rather weathered 80s-style sign and flappy awning at Cheriff. Step inside and you'll discover mid-century design, soft lighting and a blow-out seafood menu. It's all about the stranger delights of Spanish seafood (think gooseneck barnacles and sea cucumbers), ideal for a celebratory meal with a difference.

BAR CAÑETE

Map 2; Carrer de la Unió, 17, Raval; ///keeps.bicker.sheets; www.barcanete.com

Cañete gets overlooked by locals thanks to its location in Raval, where anything vaguely upmarket tends to be a bit touristy. Yet this oh-so-charming tapas bar is second-to-none for a birthday banquet. Choose between the buzzy area called Barra (meaning "bar"), where parties of cheerful pals mingle at stand-up tables, and the swankier sit-down section Mantel (meaning "tablecloth"). Wherever you park up, sharing plates of tapas with loved ones is just the ticket for a special occasion.

ROBATA

Map 4; Carrer d'Enric Granados, 55, Eixample;
///margin.reserved.pretty; www.robata.es

Enric Granados is *the* go-to street in the Eixample – you heard it here first. And though there are countless great spots here, Japanese restaurant Robata is hard to beat. The sushi and grills are exceptional, the sticky chicken wings are to die for, and the cheesecake (off-brand, we know) is out of this world. Add a selection of sakes (staff will talk you through them) and you'll be raving about Robata for weeks.

CINC SENTITS

Map 3; Carrer d'Entença, 60, Eixample; ///melons.piles.parties;
www.cincsentits.com

Looking for the meal of a lifetime? Look no further. At Cinc Sentits, chef Jordi Artal cooks a menu deeply rooted in Catalan tradition but with a wholly modern approach. The 10-course tasting menu at his two-Michelin-starred restaurant coaxes out flavours and aromas from the very best products of the season. If you're feeling really fancy, splash out on the wine pairings.

TERRAZA MARTÍNEZ

Map 3; Carretera de Miramar, 38, Montjuïc; ///helpful.mint.mimed;
www.martinezbarcelona.com

A special occasion deserves a special view, and nowhere can outdo Terraza Martínez when it comes to scenery. Suited-and-booted locals gaze out at the city, shoreline and mountains at this gorgeous spot,

After a paella feast? Remember that it's a lunchtime affair; locals never, ever eat paella for dinner.

plopped on the northeastern face of Montjuïc. The menu is a hit, too, with rich paellas, oysters and fresh fish – the perfect feast to celebrate, well, anything.

SILAN

Map 4; Carrer d'Enric Granados, 38, Eixample;
///deflect.typhoon.chop; 930 315 816

Why not save the celebration for morning? Kick off the day in style with a smashingly good brunch at Silan. The Israeli-focused, Middle Eastern bistro throngs with trendy crowds, all inhaling the fragrant punch of sumac and cumin wafting up from platters of shakshuka and beef kebabs. After you've feasted, sit back with another coffee and enjoy a heart-to-heart with your favourite people – the day is young, after all.

» **Don't leave without** tucking into the oblong Jerusalem bagel, baked that day and served with tahini, Moroccan olives and zaatar.

ESTIMAR

Map 1; Carrer de Sant Antoni dels Sombrerers, 3, Born;
///helpers.supper.mistaken; www.restaurante-estimar.com

The day's catch is displayed on ice like a centrepiece at this temple to seafood. Our top tip? If money is no object (wouldn't that be nice?), this is the place to sample some of Spain's luxury items, like barnacles harvested from the stormy coastline of Galicia. A more humble (and wallet-friendly) dish is the fried baby squid served with inky black mayo.

Raise a glass at
REKONS

Stop to *vermutea* ("drink vermouth")
and chomp on an Argentine empanada at
Rekons. The puff pastry is second to none.

4

CARRER DEL

FLORIDABLANCA

CARRER DE

COMTE BORRELL

CARRER DEL COMTE D'URGELL

RONDA DE SANT ANTONI

SANT
ANTONI

5

Finish up at
BAR RAMÓN

Ramón Estalella opened this cheery joint in 1939.
Swing by to say *hola* to his grandkids who are busy
keeping his legacy alive. Faded posters of jazz
stars line the walls, rock 'n' roll plays overhead and
the regulars tuck into crowd-pleasing tapas.

*Once an open-air food
market targeted at
hungry commuters,
today the now-covered*
Mercat de Sant Antoni
is a social hub.

Fortify yourself at
SANT ANTONI
GLORIÓS

Bag a barrel at this low-key
tapas bar, favoured by
Sant Antoni locals for its
top-notch *patatas bravas*
and cod fritters.

1

CARRER DE TAMARIT

CARRER DE MANSO

CARRER DE VILADOMAT

CARRER DEL PARLAM

2

Soak up some history at
BAR CALDERS

Catalan author Pere Calders took refuge in these walls
during the Civil War. Today Sant Antoni locals pack out the
bar and its terrace, tucking into traditional tapas and Mexican
specialities. Arrive early (around 6pm) to secure a spot.

0 metres 100
0 yards 100

AVINGUDA DEL PARAL·LEL

An evening of
tapas in Sant Antoni

Time spent in Barcelona isn't complete without an evening *tapeando* ("eating tapas"). Sitting next to Raval and Poble Sec, Sant Antoni – Barna's best-kept secret – is just the place for a bite-sized feast. The charming *barri* dates back to the 15th century but it was the opening of a food market, in 1882, that made Sant Antoni what it is today: a foodie hotspot where locals actually know one another's names. Expect family-run tapas bars, cosy bodegas and a warm welcome.

**3 Graze at
ELS SORTIDORS
DEL PARLAMENT**
Continue on to this buzzy bodega, where fancy tapas await. Our top pick? That's the quail egg and black truffle oil omelette.

1. Sant Antoni Gloriós
Carrer de Manso, 42;
934 240 628
///purses.mass.napped

2. Bar Calders
Carrer del Parlament, 25;
933 299 349
///harvest.timidly.trifle

3. Els Sortidors del Parlament
Carrer del Parlament, 53;
934 411 602
///sliding.raft.limes

4. Rekons
Carrer del Comte d'Urgell, 32; www.empanadasrekons.com
///rice.lofts.combos

5. Bar Ramón
Carrer del Comte Borrell, 81;
www.barramon.dudaone.com
///strapped.noting.birds

📍 **Mercat de Sant Antoni** ///hotdog.drivers.sparkle

DRINK

Locals live their lives in Barna's bodegas, vermuterias and cafés. Cocktails are sipped on date night, beers are clinked after work and coffees are savoured at weekends.

Vermouth Bars

Vermouth is more than a drink (a fortified wine, to be precise), it's a social occasion. On your travels through Barna you'll likely hear the phrase "fer el vermut", meaning to have an aperitif with a light snack.

BODEGA E. MARÍN

Map 4; Carrer de Milà i Fontanals, 72, Gràcia; ///exact.clever.suspend; 932 133 079

Impossibly narrow and bursting with bottles and barrels, this tiny bodega is a kitschy time capsule from another era. Gràcia locals (*graciencs*, to those in the know) inspect the curious decor – a lifetime of old photos, commemorative plates, handwritten notes and novelty calendars from years gone by – all while sipping the no-frills house vermouth (no ice, no garnish).

MORRO FI

Map 3; Carrer del Consell de Cent, 171, Eixample; ///unveils.chef.trap; www.morrofi.cat

Remember when blogs were a thing? That's how Morro Fi began: a blog run by friends celebrating all that made Barcelona's traditional bars tick. Years of painstaking research transformed into a real-life bar, Morro Fi, which soon became the city's vermouth bar *par excellence* despite being the size of a postage stamp. It's so popular that you'll spot Morro Fi's house-made vermouth across the city.

LAS VERMUDAS

Map 4; Carrer del Robí, 32, Gràcia; ///cattle.dabble.prone;
www.lasvermudas.com

Vermouth bars can be a traditional affair (we're looking at you Bodega E. Marín) but that's not the case at Las Vermudas, with its tropical decor and innovative cocktails (vermouth-based, naturally). Four friends – Andrea, Elena, Filippo and Rafael – established this Gràcia bar, today serving up their own takes on the city staple.

SENYOR VERMUT

Map 4; Carrer de Provença, 85, Eixample;
///complain.hamster.booklet; 935 328 865

If you happen to be walking through Eixample around midday at the weekend (in other words, prime vermouth time), you'll no doubt be drawn to Senyor Vermut. Punters spill out of the bar and onto the street corner, supping vermouth and chatting with uncharacteristic levels of conviviality for Barcelona. Inside you'll find row upon row of vermouth bottles, plus the owner's collection of antique seltzer bottles – another crucial element for a classic vermouth aperitif.

» **Don't leave without** sampling Senyor Vermut's *patatas bravas*, which locals claim are some of the best in the city thanks to the extra spicy sauce (or at least extra spicy by Catalan tastes).

Solo, Pair, Crowd

Whatever the occasion or number in your squad, there's a glut of lovely spots to clink a glass of vermouth.

FLYING SOLO
Nibbles for one

Sometimes a vermouth is best enjoyed with the company of a good book. Swing by neighbourhood hangout Espai Vermut to knock a couple back with your latest read. Feeling peckish? Pair your paperback with some tasty snacks. You won't want to leave.

IN A PAIR
Chat among the bottles

Hidden away on one of the Gothic Quarter's alleyways, La Cala del Vermut is an intimate spot to enjoy a natter and an aperitif amid all the bottles on sale. Why not buy one for later, too?

FOR A CROWD
A barrel of laughs

Forget booking a table for the whole gang – gather everyone around a barrel or two at Bodega Vinito in Sant Antoni instead. You'll all truly feel like locals.

LA VERMU

**Map 4; Carrer de Sant Domènec, 15, Gràcia; ///mascot.rocks.twists;
695 925 012**

Popular any day of the week, La Vermu buzzes with colleagues
gathering for an after-work drink and friends meeting for an aperitif.
Whatever the occasion, traditional *embutits* (cured meats and tinned
seafood) and creative tapas (like marinated bluefin tuna) are paired
with obligatory glasses of vermouth.

VERMUTERIA LA LOLA

Map 3; Carrer del Consell de Cent, 82, Eixample; ///fizzle.credited.launched

Sure, its decor might not have been updated since the 1980s, but
what makes La Lola special is its mixed bag of neighbourhood
residents, from vermouth-quaffing hipsters to *abuelas* with their
dinky lapdogs. Join them on the bar's southwest-facing terrace,
perfect for catching the midday sun.

» Don't leave without checking out the tapas under the bar's glass
counter – perfect for soaking up that second vermouth.

TRENCALÒS

Map 6; Carrer del Vallespir 73, Sants; ///shack.galaxies.slumped; 930 163 115

A ski-themed vermouth bar with mountain equipment arranged
across the walls: an odd concept, but somehow it works. No need to
pretend you know anything about Barcelona's favourite tipple here;
the charming staff will be more than happy to advise you on the
bar's huge range of vermouths.

Bodegas and Wine Bars

Old-school wine bars (bodegas) and their modern counterparts are central to the city's cultural heritage. This is where locals debrief on their day with a glass of wine, or fill up a bottle from the barrel to take home.

BAR SALVATGE

Map 4; Carrer de Verdi, 50, Gràcia; ///lists.contents.rewarding; www.barsalvatge.com

"Natural wines from wild winemakers" is the ethos at this hip Gràcia bar. The good people of Salvatge aren't concerned with a wine's prestige. They're more interested in the peculiar flavours that the natural winemaking process can conjure; the more obscure the better.

LO PINYOL

Map 4; Carrer del Torrent de l'Olla, 7, Gràcia; ///recovery.circle.dialect; www.lopinyol.com

Surely nothing beats sipping a glass of really good wine while thumbing through a pre-loved book. Lo Pinyol brings these two glorious things together in a charming setting: classic floor tiles,

If Lo Pinyol is full, head over the road to Can Codina, an authentic bodega that usually has space.

vintage furniture, barrels stacked up to the ceiling and a gorgeous wooden bar. You'll find the book exchange in the nook at the back (the best seat in the house).

BODEGA MANOLO

Map 6; Carrer del Torrent de les Flors, 101, Gràcia; ///grin.hello.migrate; 932 844 377

History is palpable at Bodega Manolo. The smell of damp, wine-soaked wood fills the air and the furnishings remain much as they were 100 years ago. With the vibe of a welcoming working men's club, the bodega is a far cry from the city's bougier wine bars, and all the better for it. See for yourself why locals are so loyal to the Gràcia institution and head here for a glass of well-aged, full-bodied red.

ZONA D'OMBRA

Map 1; Carrer de Salomó ben Adret, 12, Gothic Quarter; ///gateway.booth.figure; 935 005 802

In the heart of the Gothic Quarter, this unassuming wine bar doubles as a bottle shop specializing in regional and Spanish labels. Yes, you can pop in and buy a bottle to take home, but why not draw up a chair and sample a couple of the two-dozen wines available by the glass? There's also a selection of tapas, artisan cheeses and crusty bread that will stop you from leaving completely sozzled.

» Don't leave without ordering the tasting flight. For around the same price as a single glass you can sample three wines.

BAR BODEGA QUIMET

Map 4; Carrer de Vic, 23, Gràcia; ///drivers.sailors.cages; 932 184 189

The good people of Gràcia gravitate towards Bar Bodega Quimet for its good value lunch menu and old-world charm. The barrels on the walls aren't for show; wines are dispensed by the glass and litre for prices so cheerful that you might mistake them for typos. But don't call this spot "cheap" – it's one of the few remaining places where the quality-to-price ratio is still in favour of guests.

»» Don't leave without trying the famous octopus, an entire "arm" that's slowly simmered, charred and served with silky potato purée.

BODEGA MAESTRAZGO

Map 5; Carrer de Sant Pere Més Baix, 90, Born;
///ventures.singled.voting; www.bodegamaestrazgo.com

We all know that wine only gets better with time, and Bodega Maestrazgo is in itself a fine vintage. It's been in the same family for over 60 years and current owner José has three generations of wine knowledge to back him up. Swing by to pick his brains.

Try it!
WINE TASTINGS

José will teach you how to guzzle with confidence at a Bodega Maestrazgo tasting session. He focuses on Spanish wines, so you'll be able to show off your knowledge next time someone brings a Rioja to dinner.

CELLER CAL MARINO

Map 3; Carrer de Margarit, 54, Poble Sec; ///making.spurned.sides;
www.calmarino.tumblr.com

Once a fizzy drink factory, then a motorbike workshop, today Celler Cal Marino is filled to the rafters with barrels of wine. In true Barna style, empties are converted into makeshift tables. And gathered round them? Thirsty locals working to finish off the next barrel.

ELS SORTIDORS DEL PARLAMENT

Map 3; Carrer del Parlament, 53, Sant Antoni; ///sliding.raft.limes;
934 411 602

After clocking off for the day, office and home workers make for the ultra-cool bars on Parlament, a favourite of which is this snug bodega. Els Sortidors de Parlament brings together the rustic charm of an old winery with all the services of a modern wine bar. Buy a bottle to-go or bag a barrel and enjoy a glass or two in-house (for a small corkage fee).

CAN CISA

Map 1; Carrer de la Princesa, 14, Born; ///cubes.flasks.backs;
www.barbrutal.com

One of the premier natural wine bars in the city, if not Spain, Can Cisa is the front half of upscale restaurant Bar Brutal. Every week, unique, natural and "living" wines from around the world arrive at Can Cisa, and special events are held in their honour (we're talking bar takeovers, pop-up chef events and boozy brunch specials).

Coffee Shops

Like all other Europeans, Barcelonans love a good cup of coffee. And though the craze for ultra-hip coffee shops has really taken hold, the locals still cherish the city's quality old-school spots, too.

SLOW MOV

Map 4; Carrer de Luis Antúnez, 18, Gràcia; ///flagged.dirt.revives; www.slowmov.com

As the name implies, Slow Mov is hailed as the coffee version of the slow food movement. Step into this airy space for a quick dose of caffeine and, before you know it, you'll have spent an hour watching the baristas expertly roast the single-origin beans and craft frothy latte art. An unhurried coffee here really is the perfect pick-me-up.

SATAN'S COFFEE CORNER

Map 5; Gran Via de les Corts Catalanes, 700, Eixample; ///develops.bother.fixture; www.satanscoffee.com

Barna's wave of speciality coffee shops started with Satan's Coffee Corner (or SCC). Its devilishly good brews (made with beans roasted by SSC's partners in crime Right Side Coffee) were first sold out the window of a vintage store in the Raval. These days scenesters make

Take your coffee out back into Casa Bonay's "Libertine Lounge" where there are often DJ sets.

for the branch found in the chic Casa Bonay hotel. Kitted out with Scandi furnishings and plants galore, it's the place to be seen with a *cortado*.

CAFÉS EL MAGNÍFICO

**Map 1; Carrer de l'Argenteria, 64, Born; ///protests.texted.entry;
www.cafeselmagnifico.com**

Regulars have been sipping their java at El Magnífico since the 1980s when Salvador Sans opened this roastery. Sure, it might not have the style of other cafés in Barna but the coffee is top-quality and freshly ground. Expect your cappuccino to arrive in chunky china with a little biscuit on the side – just like it would have in the 80s.
» Don't leave without sampling the *shakerato* (essentially espresso shaken over ice). It feels like a cocktail but it's perfectly acceptable for breakfast and great during the hotter months.

FEDERAL CAFÉ

**Map 3; Carrer del Parlament, 39, Sant Antoni; ///sunk.belonged.archives;
931 873 607**

Federal owes its name to a small town in New South Wales, and though this Sant Antoni coffee spot gives a flavour of Oz (think avocado on toast with perfectly poached eggs, washed down with a flat white), the place is wholly European in feel. Two floors of sleek wooden furnishings, stylish locals, scattered books and magazines, plus a lovely roof garden – you could be in Amsterdam or Copenhagen.

NEWS & COFFEE

Map 5; Passeig de Sant Joan, 17, Eixample; ///tailed.dodges.skin;
www.newsandcoffee.eu

The fun folk of News & Coffee have given four old, dusty newspaper stands the hipster treatment, kitting them out with indie magazines and top-of-the-line coffee machines. Behind the counters, beanie-wearing baristas skilfully pour speciality coffees to-go and dish out zine recommends (their motto is "if you don't like to read, you haven't found the right magazine"). Just down the road from Parc de la Ciutadella (p176), the stand in Eixample is our favourite.

ON Y VA

Map 6; Carrer de Cornet i Mas, 9, Sarrià-Sant Gervasi;
///boomed.dove.swim; www.onyvacoffee.com

Coffee connoisseur and keen cyclist Ferran Buxeda is the brains behind On y va (which means "let's go" in French). Ferran knows exactly what his fellow cyclists need on a bike ride stop-off: strong speciality coffees and tasty snacks to keep them pedalling, not to mention a wonderful sense of community.

ESPAI JOLIU

Map 5; Carrer de Badajoz, 95, Poblenou; ///supplier.maximum.adopts;
www.whereplantsmeet.coffee

Espai Joliu translates as "beautiful space" and it's not a misnomer: this is one of the most picturesque coffee shops you'll find in Barna. Doubling as a concept store selling plants and ceramics (read:

hipster HQ), the Berlin-inspired, industrial-chic spot is all peeling paint and mismatched furniture, with tables dotted about its urban jungle. There's also a good stock of indie publications if you're looking for something to flick through over your flat white.

>> Don't leave without taking a stroll through the Poblenou cemetery, just around the corner, for some quiet time with your coffee.

SYRA

Map 4; Carrer de la Mare de Déu dels Desemparats, 8, Gràcia; ///kindest.pastime.payout; www.syracoffee.com

Barcelonans know that Gràcia's many squares are perfect for settling down with a coffee and indulging in a bit of people-watching. And Syra, a little hole-in-the-wall café, provides people with the perfect coffee for these moments. Single-origin, freshly roasted, aromatic: the coffee here is sublime, especially when paired with delicious treats like baklava and carrot cake.

NOMAD COFFEE LAB

Map 5; Passatge Sert, 12, Sant Pere; ///sensible.sunk.organs; www.nomadcoffee.es

No mention of coffee in Barcelona is complete without a nod to Nomad, one of the pioneers in the city's speciality coffee movement. The first of three branches, the Nomad Coffee Lab is nestled in a pretty, plant-filled passage in the upper reaches of Sant Pere. Here, founder Jordi Mestre and his team test and serve their newest and most special beans, sourced responsibly from farmers across the world.

Characterful Bars

Looking for a watering hole with a difference? Tucked down the city's ancient streets, these characterful boozers – plus their quirky owners and eccentric decor – promise a story with your drink.

LONDON BAR

Map 2; Carrer Nou de la Rambla, 34, Raval; ///outpost.nursery.wedge; www.londonbar-bar.negocio.site

When London Bar opened in the 1910s, the aim was to imitate a British pub and give punters like Dalí and Picasso (both regulars) a taste of the English capital. But something must have been lost in translation. Instead of the low wooden beams, leather armchairs and bar taps that are synonymous with British boozers, the place is a hodgepodge of Art Deco decor and fancy cocktail menus. This doesn't stop Barcelonans from popping in for a knees-up, mind.

BAR LEO

Map 5; Carrer de Sant Carles, 34, Barceloneta; ///milder.outdone.pastime

It might have been open for just 40 years but locals say you're not a true Barcelonan until you've stepped inside Bar Leo. You'll be greeted by the warm, few-toothed smile of owner Leocadia and the trill of rumba music (plus posters of flamenco legend Bambino peeling on the walls). Like an Andalucian mother, Leocadia will insist you try her *tortilla de patatas* and *banderillas* (a cocktail stick of olives, pepper and anchovies) as well as an obligatory vermouth. Don't leave anything on your plate – she'll be back to check that you enjoyed every item.

LA CONCHA

Map 2; Carrer de Guàrdia, 14, Raval; ///places.builder.galaxies; www.laconchadelraval.com

Actor and singer Sara Montiel was one of the few gay icons of Francoist Spain and this LGBTQ+ bar is dedicated to her memory. Every wall is plastered with portraits of the fearless diva, Spain's first Hollywood star who spoke out passionately for gender equality. Montiel passed away in 2013 but her spirit lives on at La Concha.

BAR MARSELLA

Map 2; Carrer de Sant Pau, 65, Raval; ///recoup.gold.warm

Dating back to 1820, Bar Marsella became notorious in the 1920s when artists and bohemians sipped absinthe here to fuel their creativity. The beloved haunt has barely been cleaned since those days; pre-Civil War bottles line the walls, the ceiling is stained with cigarette smoke and the chandeliers are thick with cobwebs. Add the surly nature of the owner and you'll feel like you've fallen into a ghost story. Or perhaps that's just the influence of the green fairy.

» **Don't leave without** settling your stomach after all that absinthe by stumbling over to La Monroe de la Filmo for some delicious tapas.

BAR OLÍMPIC

Map 2; Carrer de Joaquín Costa, 25, Raval; ///bespoke.rods.clues; 931 711 525

Oh, the 80s! A decade of hedonistic partying, Freddie Mercury and pre-Olympic fever. It was all this that inspired the opening of Bar Olímpic in the late 80s when the city was gearing up for the 1992 Olympics. Today good-timers come here for the cheap beer and revelrous vibes. Seriously, you'll be singing Freddie and Montserrat's "Barcelona" before your second beer.

BAR RAÏM

Map 4; Carrer de Siracusa, 4, Gràcia; ///sensible.loves.escape; 687 459 679

The region of Catalunya has a shady colonial history. Take the rum trade: everyone's go-to rum, Bacardí, was created by an *indià*, the name given to Catalans who made their fortune in the Caribbean, particularly in Cuba. Bar Raïm is all about spotlighting this dark patch of local history, with black-and-white photographs and Cuban flags plastered across its walls, all to remind locals of the past.

BAR PASTÍS

Map 2; Carrer de Santa Mònica, 4, Raval; ///steadily.loads.encoded; 619 753 740

Slip into the world of French writer Jean Genet at Pastís. This dinky 1940s bar was once a favourite with cabaret-goers and French exiles, such as Genet, who lived here in Barna. It's still got that feel of the Raval underworld, thanks to the portraits of bohemians, yellowing newspaper cuttings and the incongruous pair of plastic legs sporting can-can stockings (ripped, naturally). As for drinks, Gallic aperitifs are the order of the day, including the eponymous *pastís*, an aniseed spirit that turns white when you add water.

CASA ALMIRALL

Map 2; Carrer de Joaquín Costa, 33, Raval; ///blushed.vase.fishery; www.casaalmirall.com

This is *the* place to take a date, though you won't be alone; dating app matches are regulars at Casa Almirall. The front section of this 1920s gem is done up in full Art Deco flare, with a gorgeous wooden bar. The back (beyond the dividing screen), meanwhile, is decorated speakeasy-style. Settle on one of the velvet sofas, order a bottle of red and prepare to spend the evening swapping life stories with your date.

» Don't leave without ordering a couple of vermouths, which will come served with soda water from a vintage seltzer bottle.

Shh!

Fancy a sophisticated night in an old members-only smoking club? Seek out Pipa Club *(www. barcelona pipaclub.com)*, now a classy cocktail joint with DJ sets and a cohort of pool players practising their aim. Secreted behind a tiny door in a corner of Plaça Reial, in the Gothic Quarter, it's not easy to find; look for the Pipa Club plaque, ring the buzzer and keep your fingers crossed that someone answers the door.

Cocktail Joints

When they want to mix things up a bit, Barna locals make for the city's punchy cocktail bars. And, handily, the city has plenty of tempting offerings to quench their thirst.

MARLOWE BAR

Map 1; Carrer del Rec, 24, Born; ///hungry.remain.jotting; 717 702 732

Ever wondered what your cocktail of choice says about you? Marlowe Bar is here to answer that question. How? With nothing by way of a menu. Here you'll chat with expert bartenders (if you're shy, this might not be the place for you), who on sussing out your style will tailor a cocktail just for you. Expect delicious concoctions often made using foraged ingredients.

BALIUS

Map 5; Carrer de Pujades, 196, Poblenou; ///decades.tomb.instead; www.baliusbar.com

Formerly an old pharmacy of the same name, Balius is now a retro-cool vermouth and cocktail bar. Residents around the Rambla and Poblenou love this spot for its simple yet flavour-packed cocktails. Take the signature Sambac cocktail, with pisco, jasmine, camomile and citrus, or The Wall, which blends bourbon and mezcal with grapefruit and a touch of cinnamon. Come on a Sunday and sip your chosen tipple to the sounds of live jazz.

BAR BOADAS

Map 2; Carrer dels Tallers, 1, Raval; ///parties.twigs.jiggle; 933 189 592

Welcome to the oldest cocktail joint in the city. Opened in 1933 by a *coctelero* (cocktail waiter) who honed his skills serving up daiquiris in Havana, Boadas remains a bar of high pedigree – just look at the Art Deco decor, smartly suited waiters and celebrity signatures lining the walls. Yes, the bar is located in the heart of grungy Raval but the guests here are dressed to impress. Put on your finest and prepare for an evening of pure sophistication.

» Don't leave without trying the dry martini, which is infused with sandalwood and bergamot. *Deliciós.*

PESCA SALADA

Map 2; Carrer de la Cera, 32, Raval; ///tipping.invents.hears; 651 148 670

This place was once a neighbourhood salted cod shop (yes, that was a thing) and on entering you'll see that things remain a little fishy. The space is the size of a fisher's hut, scales are fastened to the ceiling, and is that a lamp in the shape of a tin of mackerel? Punters pack in like sardines for a last round of goldfish bowl-sized G&Ts before hitting the clubs. Pesca Salada really does have the locals hook, line and sinker.

DR. STRAVINSKY

Map 1; Carrer dels Mirallers, 5, Born; ///price.enter.escaping;
www.drstravinsky.cat

This cocktail laboratory could be the den of an eccentric doctor turned wizard – just look at all the bubbling beakers and jars of tinctures. The intrigue doesn't stop at the decor. Take the cocktail menu, which is out designed like an old illustration of the galaxy. Planets are labelled with types of flavour (think smoky, sour, fruity) so you can choose your perfect flavour of cocktail. Expect surprising ingredients like feta cheese, sundried tomato and even sea urchin.

COLLAGE

Map 1; Carrer dels Consellers, 4, Born; ///chatted.rent.hoofs;
www.collagecocktailbar.com

Tucked away on a quiet street, Collage is the place to hide away with a potent seasonal cocktail. Founder and bartender Fernando Requena crafts drinks around the time of year, like the autumnal Smashing Pumpkins cocktail: rye whisky, fortified wine and a spiced syrup of roasted pumpkin – the perfect warmer on a chilly night.

TWO SCHMUCKS

Map 2; Carrer de Joaquín Costa, 52, Raval; ///energy.neutron.sending;
www.schmuckordie.com

When globetrotter and cocktail aficionado Moe Aljaff set foot in Barcelona to run a couple of pop-up bars, he was forced to stay by popular demand. He set up Two Schmucks on a shoestring budget, and the bar soon skyrocketed into the World's 50 Best Bars. But things remain down to earth; the list of expletives on the door hints that this is hardly a posh spot. We are in the Raval, after all.

» Don't leave without supping one of the Curry Coladas, a creative take on the piña colada inspired by the Raval's South Asian community.

BAR PARADISO

Map 1; Carrer de Rera Palau, 4, Born; ///sank.less.between; www.paradiso.cat

Upon arriving at Bar Paradiso, you'll be met by a pastrami shop. Don't fret, you're in the right place. Step inside the shop's fridge (no codewords needed here) and find yourself in a softly lit, mid-century speakeasy with mixologists working their cocktail magic. Genuine magic. We're talking helium-infused coffee clouds perched atop coupes, and tornadoes of pisco, apple kombucha and orange blossom swirling hypnotically at the push of a button. A word to the wise: there are just 12 seats at Bar Paradiso, so get there promptly – else you'll be going home with just a pastrami sandwich.

Try it!
VERMOUTH UNIVERSITY

Don't be late for class at Vermouth University. At Las Vermudas (p61) you'll master a range of cocktail recipes using Barcelona's favourite tipple. Graduating has never been so much fun.

Orxateries and Xocolateries

No coffee, no alcohol – these charming cafés are truly unique to Barcelona. Open all year, orxateries are the go-to in summer, before xocolateries come into their own in winter.

DULCINEA

Map 1; Carrer de Petritxol, 2, Gothic Quarter; ///allergy.casual.foods; www.granjadulcinea.com

On sweet-themed Carrer Petritxol – or "chocolate street" – sits this charming *xocolateria* (pronounced *shoo-koo-luh-tuh-REE-uh*). Dulcinea is a blast from the past with its suited waiters and comforting range of traditional (and gloriously gloopy) Catalan chocolate drinks.

SIRVENT

Map 3; Carrer del Parlament, 56, Sant Antoni; ///assures.usual.ranked; www.turronessirvent.com

Ah, Sirvent. This legendary spot is one of Barna's oldest and most beloved *orxateries* (*oor-shuh-tuh-REE-uhs*). These traditional cafés are dedicated to serving the sweetened tiger nut drink *orxata*, a favourite refreshment in Spain, especially in summertime. Hordes of thirsty locals queue up to sit-in with a glass of *orxata* or fill a two-litre container to enjoy at home.

» **Don't leave without** pairing your *orxata* with a few *fartons*, which are traditional pastries akin to iced buns.

CAN SOLER
Map 6; Carrer del Mar, 97, Badalona; ///beeline.nimbly.poster; www.artesanssoler.com

When it's feeling hot hot hot, Badalona beachgoers walk just a few steps from the shore to Can Soler for a reviving fix of *orxata*. But the nutty drink isn't the only cooling treat on the menu here; Albert Soler, owner and grandson of the café's founder, has won prizes for his ice cream (no mean feat for a country that loves *gelat*). Orxata or ice cream? It's hot, have both.

GRANJA VIADER
Map 2; Carrer d'en Xuclà, 4, Raval; ///confused.referral.shady; www.granjaviader.cat

This old-world *xocolateria* also happens to be one of the few remaining *granges* (cafés specializing in dairy products) that sprang up across Barcelona in the late 19th century. In fact, the *xocolateria* still has the very marble tables that Picasso sat at to muse and drink, or so they claim. If the balmy summer months make the thought of drinking hot chocolate unbearable, you can enjoy this historic spot with a cold chocolate milk.

XOCOLATERIA LA NENA

Map 4; Carrer de Ramón y Cajal, 36, Gràcia; ///format.fakes.stencil;
www.la-nena-chocolate-cafe.business.site

A hit with Barcelonan families, "The Little Girl" is all bright colours, vintage toys and more than a whiff of chocolate. Afternoons are a little frantic, with parents bringing children in for an after-school treat, so pop by for elevenses and a read of the paper instead, for a more relaxed affair.

EL TÍO CHE

Map 5; Rambla del Poblenou, 44–46, Poblenou; ///fall.input.sprays;
www.eltioche.es

After a morning of sun on Mar Bella beach (p167), and the inevitable sweaty stroll back into the city, a visit to El Tío Che is a must. Sip a glass of *el granziado de cebada* (a malt-based slushy) out on the café terrace and you'll be ready to get back out there before you know it.

PLANELLES DONAT

Map 1; Avinguda del Portal de l'Àngel, 27, Gothic Quarter;
///selects.orange.merchant; www.planellesdonat.com

A beloved institution, Planelles Donat has been in the game since 1929. Silver-haired couples often pop into the old-school *orxateria* for a little treat after mass, sipping heavenly glasses of *orxata* at the café's long marble counter.

» Don't leave without calling in at the imposing Cathedral of Barcelona, which pre-dates the Sagrada Família by 400 years.

Liked by the locals

"We started out as a small family business some 20 years ago. We've always wanted to keep the place like a small-café, part of the fabric of the neighbourhood. We don't follow trends: we just do what we do, and do it well. All you need is cocoa and fresh milk!"

PEP CAÑAMERAS,
OWNER OF XOCOLATERIA LA NENA

An evening bar-hopping in
Gràcia's squares

Barna's squares are treated like communal backyards – places to catch up with friends and read the paper. Gràcia locals in particular appreciate their *barri*'s numerous *plaças*, which have retained a charming, villagey feel (Gràcia was a town before it was absorbed into the city in the 1800s). Lined with age-old bodegas and *vermuterias*, these public spaces are ideal for pulling up a chair, enjoying a few tipples and watching the world go by.

1. Bar Virreina
Plaça de la Virreina, 1;
934 153 209
///splash.protect.mainland

2. Bar Canigó
Carrer de Verdi, 2;
www.barcanigo.com
///composed.zoom.waddled

3. Sol Soler
Plaça del Sol, 21
///tenses.observes.stump

4. Bar Bodega Quimet
Carrer de Vic, 23;
932 184 189
///drivers.sailors.cages

5. Mustà Shawarma
Carrer de Mozart, 4;
935 008 591
///inches.graced.strict

Plaça del Diamant ///recently.teachers.stretch

Plaça de la Vila de Gràcia ///puns.parrot.candles

PLAÇA DE LA
VIRREINA

1

Begin with a snack at
BAR VIRREINA

Don't let Bar Virreina's
laminated menu deter you:
these guys do the best
bocadillos (sandwiches) on
Plaça de la Virreina.

PLAÇA DEL
DIAMANT

In **Plaça del Diamant**
*stands a statue of the
protagonist from Mercè
Rodoreda's novel that
took its name from this
very square.*

2

Step back in time at
BAR CANIGÓ

Order a vermouth at Bar Canigó.
Before the war, the owner's grandfather
sold a glass of the good stuff for less
than a *peseta*. It's pricier these days,
but served just as it was back then.

GRÀCIA

PLAÇA
DEL SOL

3

Soak up the scene in
SOL SOLER

Order a beer and some *patatas
bravas* at Sol Soler and watch
buskers perform for the crowds
milling about in Plaça del Sol.

**Plaça de la Vila de
Gràcia** *is home to the
barri's emblematic clock
tower and has been the
setting of everything
from revolts to weddings.*

PLAÇA
DE LA VILA
DE GRACIA

Finish up at
MUSTÀ SHAWARMA

5

End the night at this
family-run Syrian spot,
famed for its shawarma with
spicy-as-hell hot sauce.

PLAÇA
DE GAL·LA
PLACÍDIA

Raise a glass at
BAR BODEGA
QUIMET

4

Run by two brothers, Bar
Bodega Quimet serves wine
from the barrel. Stop in at
this characterful old-timer
for a glass of red.

PLACETA DE
SANT MIQUEL

0 metres   200

0 yards   200

SHOP

Eco-conscious fashion, pre-loved vinyl and handmade homeware: you need only glimpse Barna's shopping scene to see that this is a city of movers, shakers and makers.

Vintage Gems

Barna has been setting trends for decades. Today young fashionistas pay homage to those who came before them by adding vintage pieces to their wardrobes. Here are some of their favourite shops.

COTTON VINTAGE
Map 4; Carrer d'Enric Granados, 26, Eixample; ///paints.ever.copycat; www.cottonvintage.es

Shopping vintage needn't involve foraging through piles of old Hawaiian shirts and moth-eaten cardigans. Take Cotton Vintage, where stock – think Christian Dior sunglasses, Manolo Blahnik stilettos and Versace coats – is neatly arranged throughout. It's all thanks to the team of Carrie Bradshaw-esque collectors, who know the story behind every luxury item. High-end fashion without hurting the planet? ¡Olé!

HUMANA VINTAGE
Map 1; Avinguda de Francesc Cambó, 30–36, Born; ///cubes.answer.drilled; www.humana-spain.org

Spain's main chain of charity shops, Humana stocks run-of-the-mill clothing donated by those enjoying a good clear-out. Humana Vintage, on the other hand, carefully selects and displays the most

Humana stores run regular sales, with items going for as little as €1. Check social media for dates.

striking donations, appealing to Barna's famously fashionable locals. Vintage shell suit? Oh yes. Jazzy shirts? Of course. Leather briefcases? Look no further.

L'ARCA

Map 1; Carrer dels Banys Nous, 20, Gothic Quarter; ///late.files.diggers; www.larcabarcelona.com

The grande dame of Barcelona's vintage scene, L'Arca is more atelier than second-hand store. A team of specialist seamstresses have been restoring and reworking delicate fabrics here since 1980. Ever swooned over Kate Winslet's wardrobe in *Titanic*? Well, a lot of her gowns were restored at this stunningly curated boutique. Lovers of old-world glamour are regulars here, fingering the antique kimonos, Spanish Manila shawls and flowing linen dresses.

» **Don't leave without** checking out the selection of wedding dresses; there are some truly elegant gowns here, at wallet-friendly prices.

PETIT ENCANTS

Map 5; Carrer de les Basses de Sant Pere, 24, Sant Pere; ///bumps.switched.gave; 933 193 151

Looking to refurbish your flat? Petit Encants is here for you. Crammed with one-of-a-kind treasures and antiques, like wrought-iron streetlamps, gilded grandfather clocks and mahogany sea chests, this relic harks back to the Barcelona of the history books. In essence, Zara Home has got nothing on this cave of wonders.

TRASH CLOSET

Map 2; Carrer dels Taller, 28, Raval; ///unique.historic.hurry; 936 739 357

One man's trash is another man's treasure, as the saying goes. Take, Trash Closet, where clubbers and drag performers find maximalist garms to create a lewk worthy of a runway. Expect second-hand tie-dye, grungy boots and sparkly jumpsuits for just a few euros.

HOLALA! PLAÇA

Map 2; Carrer de Valldonzella, 2, Raval; ///plug.random.craters;
www.holala-ibiza.com

Whichever area of Barna you're in, chances are you'll mingle with locals kitted out in pre-loved fashion from Holala! Plaça. The team here have been handpicking pieces from flea markets since 1972. Pop into the store for a browse and, an hour later, you'll stumble out with a dapper trouser suit – and a fetching leather suitcase to take it home in.

LA PRINCIPAL RETRO & CO

Map 2; Carrer de Ferlandina, 37, Raval; ///trendy.circular.crowbar;
www.laprincipalretro.com

Everyone knows it: the 1990s are back. But in a city obsessed with its Olympic heritage, did they ever really go away? La Principal Retro & Co stocks original 90s pieces that will make you feel truly nostalgic: snazzy tracksuits, flashy designer jeans, oversized bomber jackets. It's like the Spice Girls are top of the charts again.

» Don't leave without following Barna's hipsters by picking up one of the store's totes, inspired by Russian posters for the 1992 Olympics.

FLAMINGOS VINTAGE KILO

**Map 2; Carrer dels Tallers, 68, Raval; ///writing.cheered.locating;
www.vintagekilo.com**

North American fashion is the name of the game at vintage empire
Flamingos, which bursts at the seams with pieces sourced in Texas,
NYC and Los Angeles. It's this branch that keeps Barna's students
coming back again and again, thanks to the best selection of 80s
sports gear, 90s sweaters and vintage Vans – all on sale by the kilo.

LULLABY VINTAGE

**Map 2; Carrer de la Riera Baixa, 22, Raval; ///changes.hunter.stunner;
934 430 802**

The crowning jewel of vintage hotspot Carrer de la Riera Baixa,
Lullaby Vintage attracts eagle-eyed magpies with glittering displays of
costume jewellery from bygone eras. If you can, come on a Saturday
afternoon when the street transforms into an alfresco vintage market.

One of Barcelona's oldest train
stations, Estació de França, in
Born, sometimes plays host to
vintage market Lost&Found
(www.lostfoundmarket.com).
The station foyer fills out with
local fashion hoarders trying to
free up space in their wardrobes
by selling their garms; some
fashion-laden stalls even spill
out onto the platforms. There's
always some food stalls to keep
energy levels up. Oh, and a
vermouth bar, of course.

Book Nooks

Catalans love books so much that on 23 April – the day of Catalunya's patron saint (Sant Jordi) – they exchange books and roses. This adoration for the written word translates to Barna's bookshop scene.

LAIE CCCB

Map 2; Plaça dels Àngels, 1, Raval; ///cutaway.unrealistic.frost; www.laie.es

After exploring the CCCB *(p129)* – one of the city's most important cultural centres – art and design students quench their creative thirst at the centre's bookshop. Laie CCCB lives up to its privileged location, with gorgeous coffee table books dedicated to art, cinema and cultural theory arranged oh-so artfully (almost too pretty to touch, in fact).

ALTAÏR

Map 4; Gran Via de les Corts Catalanes, 616, Eixample; ///heeding.poet.hamper; www.altairviatges.com

You're holding this book in your hands so we reckon you're a fellow traveller. Sate your wanderlust at Altaïr, Barcelona's specialist travel book emporium. Spread across two floors, and decorated with globes and suitcases, here you'll discover travel writing for every

Altaïr has a message board where you can post info about a trip you're planning or find a travel buddy.

destination under the sun. Pick up a guidebook and start planning your next getaway in the basement café – we'll see you there.

LA RAPOSA

Map 3; Carrer de Tapioles, 47, Poble Sec; ///divide.rinses.above; www.laraposacoop.org

This one is so much more than just a bookshop – it's a community. Founded by three friends, Moma, Alba and Nat, cooperative La Raposa is a social space for sharing feminist and queer ideas. Naturally it's also one of the best stores in Barcelona to pick up a book on these subjects. After buying a tome or two, grab a drink at the shop's café; you'll find yourself in deep discussion with local activists, intellectuals and plucky rebels before you know it.

» Don't leave without tucking into the vegan set menu out in La Raposa's garden – the perfect fuel to start your new book.

LA CENTRAL

Map 4; Carrer de Mallorca, 237, Eixample; ///nests.enforced.farm; www.lacentral.com

Shadow of the Wind fans: there's something Cemetery-of-Forgotten-Books-like about La Central, with its endless wooden bookcases and creaking floorboards. But the real magic lies in the store's gorgeous stone-walled and fairy-lit patio garden – the ideal place to get lost in a book.

MARCAPÁGINAS

Map 3; Carrer de Llançà, 32, Eixample; ///empty.posts.surveyed; 931 630 515

Learning Catalan? Looking to improve your Spanish? Consider brushing up with a graphic novel (a picture says a thousand words, after all). Tucked away behind Plaça Espanya, this tiny temple to the graphic novel is the best place to pick up a thrilling read that won't have you constantly reaching for an online translator.

LATA PEINADA

Map 2; Carrer de la Verge, 10, Raval; ///starters.motel.tides;
www.latapeinada.com

Barcelona has been the publishing capital of the Hispanosphere for a century, and this bookshop celebrates the fact. Lovers of all things Latin American are regulars at Lata Peinada's book events, workshops, concerts and annual LatAm literature festival.

The University of Barcelona is found right in the city centre, a setting that reflects education being at the very heart of Catalan identity. But few visitors realise that its university library is also open to them. Enter and you'll find literature students nose-deep in books, maths students jabbing feverishly at calculators and shelves of tomes that have survived centuries. Take it all in before heading to the lovely gardens, where you'll make friends with the countless cats who call them home.

HIBERNIAN

Map 4; Carrer del Montseny, 17, Gràcia; ///school.purest.sounds;
www.hibernianbooks.com

If you're the kind of reader who covets the smell of an old book, look no further: you've found nirvana. Second-hand bookshop Hibernian specializes in English-language books, with many going for under €5; trade in an old novel and the lovely staff will even give you a discount.

» Don't leave without taking your purchase over to Plaça de la Revolució to enjoy the book and square in their full glory.

LLIBRERIA CÓMPLICES

Map 1; Carrer de Cervantes, 4, Gothic Quarter; ///minds.piles.splits;
www.libreriacomplices.com

This LGBTQ+ bookshop was the first of its kind in Barcelona when it opened in 1994, and continues to fly the flag (literally: there's a huge rainbow flag hanging above the door). Snuggled down one of the Gothic Quarter's side streets, this pocket-sized store is stuffed-full of books covering queer theory, fiction and poetry in various languages.

FINESTRES

Map 4; Carrer de la Diputació, 249, Eixample; ///strut.communal.jolly;
www.llibreriafinestres.com

New kid on the block Finestres opened in 2021 as a place to read books, not just buy them. Plush sofas pepper the stylish store, tempting locals (and their dogs) to kick back with a paperback and swap recommends in hushed whispers with the bookworm sat next to them.

Home Touches

Barcelonans are a stylish bunch and this doesn't stop at their wardrobes. Locally woven baskets, artisanal ceramics and hand-poured candles make a home here. And you can buy a bit of Barna to take home, too.

BON VENT

Map 1; Carrer de l'Argenteria, 41, Born; ///costumes.regime.saga; www.bonvent.cat

It doesn't get more Mediterranean than Bon Vent, a concept store that has all the vibes of a chic villa on Spain's southern coast. Artisanal wares include pretty glassware, wicker baskets and hand-painted tiles. Perfect pieces for bringing a little gust of fresh sea air into your city flat.

RAIMA

Map 1; Carrer Comtal, 27, Gothic Quarter; ///deny.weeks.petition; www.raima.cat

Home workers wanting to beautify their office space can't resist Raima. The six-storey stationery Shangri-la stocks 3,000 types of paper (who knew there were so many?), plus colour-coded displays of notebooks, fancy fountain pens and classy desk planners – everything needed to make working from home a bit more cheerful.

ESPARTERIA LLUCH

Map 3; Gran Via de les Corts Catalanes, 339, Sants;
///reserved.gloves.dribble; www.esparterialluch.wordpress.com

A far cry from the pricey design stores that self-proclaimed style mavens go weak at the knees for, this cavern is one of the city's few remaining handmade wicker and woven *esparto* grass specialists. You could spend hours here, rummaging through the teetering stacks to get your hands on that perfect wicker fruit bowl or picnic basket.

» Don't leave without learning more about local design at nearby Poble Espanyol, Barcelona's open-air architectural museum.

GREY STREET

Map 2; Carrer del Peu de la Creu, 25, Raval;
///passions.assemble.tutored; www.greystreetbarcelona.com

With a bit of everything, Grey Street is just the place for sniffing out a gift, especially when you don't know where to begin. Everything this quirky concept store stocks – ceramics, planters, tea towels – is artsy and within your budget. Rest assured you won't leave empty-handed.

Try it!
PHOTOGRAPHY ART

Prefer to hang your own artwork on the wall? Head to Lomography in Born to learn camera basics and printing techniques, or attend a street photography session (*www.microsites.lomography.com*).

CASA ATLÂNTICA

**Map 4; Carrer de la Llibertat, 7, Gràcia; ///secretly.sometime.splice;
www.casaatlantica.es**

Traditional artisanal pieces are a hit with Barna's cool crowd, especially those from Casa Atlântica. Designers Belén and Lester scour flea markets in Galicia to unearth forgotten household wares that they then return to their former glory. These treasures sit alongside locally crafted items, like rugs, jugs and planters, all of which have a similarly rustic feel. It's all about traditional craftsmanship and paying respect to the past – needless to say, we're big fans.

LA NOSTRA CIUTAT

**Map 1; Carrer del Pi, 11, Gothic Quarter; ///callers.mankind.across;
www.lanostraciutat.co**

Follow in the footsteps of the design-forward locals and update your living room's walls with a print from La Nostra Ciutat. Showcasing works by local painters, illustrators and designers, the shop is awash with colour and artistic styles. Better yet, the prices are wallet-friendly.

CERERÍA ABELLA

**Map 2; Carrer de Sant Antoni Abat, 9, Raval; ///darting.nodded.supper;
www.candles.barcelona**

Looking for a little piece of history to take home? It was 1862 when, following the death of her father, Francesca Abella left her village in the Pyrenees for Barcelona. Here she opened a candle shop to serve the homes and churches (her main client) of Raval. The charismatic entrepreneur lit the way for her niece, María Abella, to oversee the business during the Civil War. Today, over a century later, the shop remains in the family and is still going strong, with droves of devoted locals stocking up on scented candles of all colours, shapes and sizes. Francesca would be proud.

GANIVETERIA ROCA

Map 1; Plaça del Pi, 3, Gothic Quarter; ///hamster.forecast.field; www.ganiveteriaroca.com

Aspiring chefs: we've one for you. This knife emporium (*ganivet* means knife in Catalan) has kept Barcelonans' kitchen drawers well-stocked since 1911. You'll find every kind of sharp implement here: chopping knives, Japanese *sashimi* knives, kitchen gadgets, plus pocket knives, scissors, shaving kits – the list goes on. Extra points for also having the most incredible window display in the city.

» Don't leave without a pair of the housebrand multi-use kitchen shears. They're truly cutting-edge (ahem), and will remind you of Barcelona with every snip of butcher's twine or pop of a bottle top.

HEY SHOP

Map 2; Carrer del Dr Dou, 4, Raval; ///garden.lure.swept; www.heyshop.es

You'll likely spot locals sporting Hey tote bags as they go about their lives – the graphic branding is instantly recognizable, thanks to its colourful, typographic design. Stop by the bricks-and-mortar shop to grab one for yourself, or peruse the posters and prints emblazoned with colourful, geometric lettering.

Record Shops

In a city where club nights segue into morning raves, and summer festival weekends are spent dancing in the sun, record shops are holy ground. Here locals rifle through vinyl for their favourite DJ's latest sounds.

BARCELONA CITY RECORDS

Map 5; Carrer d'En Mònec, 13, Born; ///securing.jungle.renews; 666 118 347

Locals know that they're in safe hands at Barcelona City Records, which is headed up by the groovy folks of Marula Café *(p146)*, famous for its vinyl-only club nights. This bright and airy spot specializes in pre-loved disco, soul, funk and Latin albums from the 60s and 70s. Deep disco addicts are repeat customers, sniffing out hard-to-find albums that will make their vinyl-obsessed friends green with envy.

DISCOS PARADISO

Map 2; Carrer de Ferlandina, 39, Raval; ///climate.smug.logged; www.discosparadiso.com

There's no getting away from it: 20- and 30-something Barcelonans are all about electronic music. When payday arrives, they converge at this music powerhouse, rubbing shoulders with DJs playing at Razzmatazz *(p144)* or Primavera Sound. Everyone rifles dexterously through the crates of new and second-hand records, their eyes darting over house, techno, jungle and synthpop vinyl. Having selected a record, music aficionados take advantage of the store's listening deck to try before they buy – though most know they're guaranteed a banger whatever they've picked up.

ULTRA-LOCAL RECORDS

Map 5; Carrer de Pujades, 113, Poblenou; ///cities.elevate.fairy; www.ultralocalrecords.blogspot.com

It's all about celebrating Catalan artists and Barcelona-based labels at Ultra-Local. And who knew there were so many? Under the cheery bunting strung across the ceiling, row upon row of crates are stuffed-full with regional albums, LPs and EPs. A record that transports you back to Barna? There's no better souvenir than that.

» Don't leave without showing your support to local artists by sticking around for a live promotional performance.

TVINYL

Map 2; Carrer de Valldonzella, 25, Raval; ///dabble.unit.couple; www.tvinyl.myshopify.com

With over 30 years' experience in the music business, Jerome "Tvinyl" Dessolier has made it his mission to spread love and music at his shop in Raval. He's a force of nature; give him the lowdown on your music preferences and he'll scour his store to unearth new sounds just for you (house, garage, disco, techno – he knows it all). Bulldog Lola will also likely come and say hello.

REVÓLVER RECORDS

Map 2; Carrer dels Tallers, 11, Raval; ///props.kitchen.insiders;
www.revolverrecords.es

Yellowing gig posters plastered across the walls, peeling black paint
and a larger-than-life mural of 70s rockstars KISS: Revólver Records
has all the trimmings of an old-school record store. But it's not just
the stomping ground of old rockers; the store's extensive collection
of electronic, goth and punk attracts young musos too.

» Don't leave without popping next door to sister store Discos
Revólver for indie favourites.

JAZZ MESSENGERS

Map 4; Carrer de Còrsega, 202, Eixample; ///trumpet.coughed.into;
www.jazzmessengers.com

Thanks to its semi-basement location and smooth soundtrack, Barna's
go-to for jazz and soul could have been plucked from the streets of
NYC. Like in any good speakeasy, the staff are only too happy to
make your visit extra special by dishing out recommendations,
including music-themed books to pair with your vinyl.

ESPAI SALVADISCOS

Map 3; Plaça de Santa Madrona, 4, Poble Sec; ///muddle.vocally.ranks;
www.salvadiscos.co

The name here literally translates as "album saver", which
explains the lifebuoy hanging incongruously in the middle of the
shop. The passionate team at Salvadiscos save unwanted records

from the attics and cellars of spring-cleaning grandparents and from boxes of junk thrown out on the street (sacrilege, we know). Given the store's unorthodox methods of sourcing music, Barcelona's vinyl junkies hit up this chocolate box of curiosities safe in the knowledge there's always something unique on offer.

EL GENIO EQUIVOCADO
Map 4; Carrer de Benet Mercadé, 22, Gràcia; ///points.totally.february; www.labotiga.elgenioequivocado.com

We can think of worse ways to spend an hour or two than in the company of DJs Pin&Pon – Joan and Rafa to their friends – at El Genio Equivocado. With their own record label of the same name, the duo kit out this stylish shop with indie records, cassettes and CDs (all old and new), plus books on music and queer culture, and branded merch. Best of all? The partners in life, music and business host vermouth-fuelled live music events here in store.

Don't miss shopping arcade Galeries Olímpia, in Sant Antoni *(Ronda de Sant Pau, 17)*, where you'll discover four little-known second-hand record stores: Globe Records Shop, Vinilarium, Crokan's Mutant Store and Rhythm Control. They're tiny but the best things come in small packages, right? All four stores open at 3pm and, handily, the arcade bar opens at 5pm. Happy digging!

Indie Clothing Stores

Yes, Barcelona is one of the world's fashion capitals but the city is also making waves with its independently owned fashion stores and eco-conscious clothing lines. Feel-good fashion with a heart? Viva Barcelona!

ANGLE STORE

Map 1; Carrer dels Mirallers, 10, Born; ///cobras.sticky.pads;
www.anglestore.com

In the fight against fast fashion, Angle Store creates clothing that is both timeless in style and long-lasting in quality. An architect by trade, store owner and designer Claudia Roca applies the principles of modular design to clothing, creating practical and easy-to-match pieces in minimalist shapes and colours.

AVEC STUDIO

Map 6; Carrer d'Amigó, 39, Sarrià-Sant Gervasi; ///dish.misfits.blazers;
www.avec-studio.com

Leading the way in the slow-fashion scene, Avec Studio's Inés and Alejandro are all about making clothes ethically and responsibly. Everything is solely designed and produced here in Barna, so you can expect great craftsmanship and no air miles.

BLAW STORE

Map 5; Carrer del Bruc, 22, Eixample; ///dome.slogged.about;
www.blawstore.com

Self-proclaimed "House of Men" BLAW Store is dedicated to
curating every aspect of a man's life (food, hygiene, home decor,
fashion: you name it, they've got it). Its house labels offer
understated, quality basics at good prices, which sit alongside
in-demand names like Deus, Denham and Patagonia.

BRAVA FABRICS

Map 3; Carrer del Parlament, 21, Sant Antoni; ///residual.items.folds;
www.bravafabrics.com

Imagine all the tropes of hipster life: avocados, vermouth, coffee.
Brava Fabrics has embraced these motifs across its shirt patterns,
because why be ashamed of things we like? Catering to both men
and women, Brava is committed to using eco-friendly materials, too.

>> Don't leave without making like a hipster and ordering a flat white
at Sant Antoni's Federal Café *(p69)*, just down the road.

LASER

Map 2; Carrer del Dr Dou, 2, Raval; ///cared.parkway.copiers;
www.laser-bcn.com

Laser pays homage to its home – a hub of culture, art and diversity –
by collaborating with street artists and illustrators to create the "Rawal
Artists" collection. The dedicated team controls the whole process,
from designing to distributing clothing, no middlemen in sight.

Liked by the locals

"I always dreamed of studying design in Barcelona and presenting at fashion week – to be part of the Barcelona fashion scene. It's a city where creativity and the fashion industry have always worked hand-in-hand, where you can find high-end brands alongside stores run by young designers."

RUBÉN GÓMEZ, JEWELLERY DESIGNER

TOPMANTA

Map 2; Carrer d'en Roig, 13, Raval; ///driver.supplier.timeless;
www.manteros.org

You'll likely notice the sale of sunglasses and accessories on the city's pavements; this is the *topmanta* trade, largely driven by undocumented migrants from the African diaspora. In recent years, the *manteros* (street sellers) established a syndicate to protect their rights. Before they knew it, they'd set up this store in Raval, showcasing the locally made collection "Legal Clothing, Illegal People". Locals are chuffed to see it, as all profits go towards anti-racism causes.

LADYLOQUITA

Map 4; Travessera de Gràcia, 126, Gràcia; ///drip.cleans.prone;
www.ladyloquita.com

Wooden beams, a chesterfield sofa, plants galore – this Gràcia boutique feels like owner Laura's vintage-chic flat (you won't want to leave). Yes, on-brand styles are displayed at Ladyloquita, but only those styles that are on-brand for Laura: sustainable and locally designed.

PITAGORA

Map 5; Carrer de Llull, 27, Poblenou; ///deflect.effort.logs; www.pitagora.es

Talk to any Barcelonan and they'll tell you that Poblenou is Barna's design district. And it's here you'll find clothing shop Pitagora. This spot has dropped the constructs of gender and designed all its clothes to fit and suit anybody and everybody, with simple designs and natural colours.

Gourmet Treats

Barcelona is a foodie's paradise and it doesn't stop at restaurants. Around every corner you'll find tempting artisan food shops and markets, ripe with edible treats just waiting to be devoured.

VILA VINITECA "LA TECA"
Map 1; Carrer dels Agullers, 9, Born; ///spotty.prance.invite;
www.vilaviniteca.es

Facing sister wine shop Vila Viniteca, gourmet grocer "La Teca" is the ultimate place to stock up ahead of a dinner party. Fill your basket with cured meats, canned seafoods and premium cheeses (there are 300 to choose from). It's not cheap but your guests will thank you.

Not sure what wine to serve to your friends with dinner? Book a private wine tasting at "La Teca". In the grocer's gorgeous 15th-century stone cellar you'll sample various wines plus food products to go alongside them, all with the advice and expertise of the store's staff.

LA BOQUERIA

Map 2; La Rambla, 91, Raval; ///mushroom.promotes.perkily; www.boqueria.barcelona

Barcelonans joke that if you can't find an ingredient at La Boqueria then you need to change your recipe. Early in the morning, before the throngs of *guiris* (tourists) arrive, they descend on the city's most famous food market, armed with their shopping lists and canvas shopping bags. They enter via the back and side entrances (the front entrance is used by *guiris*), knowing that it's in these hidden corners that they'll find the market's finest wild mushrooms, *jamón*, wheels of cheese and tins of saffron.

» Don't leave without stopping for lunch at the legendary El Quim de la Boqueria. Up at the restaurant's counter, you'll tuck into traditional tapas, all made from ingredients sourced here in the market.

MERCAT DE SANTA CATERINA

Map 1; Avinguda de Francesc Cambó, 16, Santa Caterina; ///decrease.propose.belts; www.mercatdesantacaterina.com

Barcelona's second most famous food market, Mercat Santa Caterina stands on the site of the medieval Convent of Saint Catherine (you'll find the archaeological site at the back of the market). The food hall has long kept city workers well-fed, first in the 19th century, when the market building was constructed, and now in the 21st. Museum staff and local professionals weave through the stalls and vendors on their lunch breaks, eyeing up the kaleidoscopic displays of fruit, buckets of olives and dishes of paella – just like those who came before them.

LA BOTIFARRERIA DE SANTA MARIA

Map 1; Carrer de Santa Maria, 4, Born; ///command.credit.proceeds;
www.labotifarreria.com

Pork is king here in Barcelona; insist a meat-eating local names their favourite type and they'll say *botifarra* (a white sausage and Catalan speciality). This beloved *botifarreria* in Born has one of the most varied assortments of house-made *botifarras* in the city. Choose from a range of ready-to-grill sausages, stuffed with tasty morsels like dates, gruyère or stewed cuttlefish – great on the go or for a dinnertime treat.

» **Don't leave without** buying a few cooked sausages prepared with black truffle – the perfect addition to an alfresco feast.

LA CHINATA

Map 1; Passeig del Born, 11, Born; ///acute.units.shelter; www.lachinata.es

Never underestimate the power of the humble olive – gourmet and cosmetics shop La Chinata certainly doesn't. The small chain store is a hotspot for initiated regulars, who come to stockpile olive oils and spreads before topping up their toiletry bags with olive oil soaps, bath gels and room sprays.

XOCOLATES FARGAS

Map 1; Carrer del Pi, 16, Gothic Quarter; ///sometime.early.token;
www.xocolatesfargas.cat

Confectioner Fargas has been charming the masses with its stone-ground chocolate since 1827 and you can still see its 200-year-old mill in action today. Treat yourself to a trademark bar of chocolate

Visit the Chocolate Museum for more cocoa joy. Tickets even come wrapped around a chocolate bar.

and, for your pals back home, buy some bags of *Catanies*, a Catalan sweet made from roasted marcona almonds set inside balls of white chocolate praline.

ENTRE LATAS

Map 4; Carrer de Torrijos, 16, Gràcia; ///pizza.holdings.civil;
www.entrelatas-bcn.com

If there's one staple foodstuff you'll find in every Catalan kitchen, it's gourmet tinned food, or *conserves*. We're talking canned fish, pâtés, vegetables – basically anything that pairs with a beer or vermouth. Entre Latas owner Paola Fornasaro is a graphic designer turned foodie hero and prides herself on curating tempting and beautifully packaged *conserves* that won't stay in your cupboard for long. Easily packable, and pretty to boot, these are the perfect Barcelonan goodies to take home.

CASA CAROT

Map 1; Carrer de la Dagueria, 16, Gothic Quarter;
///puppets.snooze.behind; 606 739 093

When Barcelonans are buying provisions for a sun-drenched picnic in Parc de la Ciutadella *(p176)*, they call in at this conveniently (read: lethally) placed artisan cheese shop. Casa Carot prides itself on small-production Catalan cheeses, all made from well-treated animals – producers are often found in store giving talks and tastings (check social media for dates).

PLAÇA DE
JAUME
SABARTÉS

Rest your feet at
GRASSHOPPER
RAMEN BAR

Recharge with a tasty bowl of
ramen and locally brewed craft
beer at Grasshopper.

Update your look at
OSCAR H GRAND

Clothing designer Oscar is all about
creative freedom, quality and elegance.
Visit his workshop and store and try on some
of his gorgeous jackets and overshirts.

4

PLAÇA DE
LA LLANA

CARRER DEL POU
DE LA CADENA

LA PRINCESA

CARRER DE LA BARRA DE FERRO

5

CARRER DE MONTCADA

BORN

CARRER DE

CARRER

CARRER DELS COTONERS

CARRER DELS
VIGATANS

CARRER DELS BANYS VELLS

CARRER DELS SOMBRERERS

Get creative at
TERRA I PELL

Feeling inspired? Join a
ceramics, jewellery or
leather-making class with
tutors Puri and Victor at
their arts studio.

6

Browse for a gift at
LASTUPENDA

Wind down the narrow
streets to this little store,
which stocks handmade,
upcycled and vegan
clothing and accessories.

3

Support local design at
IVORI

Discover young Barcelonan
designers at Ivori, a clothing
store that takes a chance on
local talent with a curated
selection of garments.

2

CARRER DELS MIRALLERS

*Born's streets are named
after items crafted here
in the 15th and 16th
centuries, like **Carrer
dels Mirallers** – the
street of mirrors.*

VIA LAIETANA

PLAÇA
DE SANTA
MARIA

0 metres   50
0 yards   50

PLAÇA DE
VÍCTOR
BALAGUER

An afternoon of
artisan shopping

*Before it thronged with shoppers, **Passeig del Born** was the execution ground for victims of the 15th-century Spanish Inquisition.*

PASSEIG DEL BORN

CARRER DE L'ESPARTERIA

CARRER DE L'ESPARTERIA

**Visit the workshop of
ALEXIS FASOLI**
Pop by Alexis Fasoli's atelier boutique to see how he creates leather accessories by hand, using traditional techniques.

PLA DE
PALAU

Early inhabitants of Born (one of the oldest *barris* in Barcelona) were fishers and labourers but, as time passed, noblemen and wealthy merchants settled here. With them grew an appetite for craftsmanship, and so skilled makers seized the opportunity to set-up shop here. Fast forward to today and these medieval streets remain the domain of local artisans and indie boutiques.

1. Alexis Fasoli
Carrer de la Volta dels Tamborets, 4;
www.alexisfasoli.com
///walking.sake.friction

2. Ivori
Carrer dels Mirallers, 7;
www.ivoribarcelona.com
///beams.puffed.overhaul

3. LaStupenda
Carrer dels Vigatans, 6;
935 256 439
///brochure.foam.flaking

4. Grasshopper Ramen Bar
Plaça de la Llana, 9;
930 178 484
///cashew.swan.audio

5. Oscar H Grand
Carrer de la Barra de Ferro, 7;
www.oscarhgrand.com
///cherub.restless.reboot

6. Terra i Pell
Carrer dels Banys Vells, 17;
https://terraipell.com
///runners.ended.bumping

📍 **Passeig del Born** ///steroids.almost.wink

📍 **Carrer dels Mirallers** ///others.nuance.worked

ARTS & CULTURE

Catalunya's cosmopolitan capital swells with creativity. This is a city built on international aspirations and local inclinations, where old and new live side by side.

City History

*If you want to better understand Catalan pride,
you need only look to the history of its capital.
Barcelona has known tragedy, but from the ashes
of war and oppression it's risen triumphant.*

NATIONAL LIBRARY OF CATALUNYA

**Map 2; Carrer de l'Hospital, 56, Raval; ///gates.measures.ozone;
www.bnc.cat**

If there's an impressive building in Barcelona that you don't know
the name of, chances are it's a library. This is a nation of bibliophiles,
after all, and Barna locals have 60 public libraries to choose from.
Their favourite? The National Library, of course. This literary temple
occupies the beautiful 15th- to 18th-century buildings of the Old
Hospital de la Santa Creu, where Gaudí died in 1926.

BARCELONA CIVIL WAR TOUR

**Map 4; Plaça de Catalunya, Eixample; ///danger.pelting.tunnel;
www.thespanishcivilwar.com**

Spain strangely doesn't have a permanent museum space dedicated
to the Civil War, in spite of cities such as Barcelona bearing its scars. It
makes sense, then, to book a walking tour with historian Nick Lloyd,

Civil War bunker Refugi 307 opens on Sunday mornings. Book a tour on the council website.

who knows all there is to know about the Second Spanish Republic and the arrival of the Franco regime. Prefer to go it alone? Turn to page 136 for a condensed tour.

CASTELL DE MONTJUÏC

Map 3; Carretera de Montjuïc, 66, Montjuïc; ///bikers.proud.locate; www.barcelona.cat/castelldemontjuic

Built by Catalan loyalists, this 17th-century fortress has seen countless revolts and wars, especially in the region's fight for independence. Today, families hosting out-of-town friends traipse around the castle grounds and exhibits, learning about the anarchists who met their fate in the castle's chilling dungeons.

» Don't leave without continuing on to Montjuïc Cemetery. It's a beautiful spot and its views are second to none.

MONESTIR DE PEDRALBES

Map 6; Baixada del Monestir 9, Pedralbes; ///followers.army.vivid; www.monestirpedralbes.barcelona

Churches dot every street corner in Barna, prompting folk to pray between running errands and cooking lunch. These holy spaces are as much a part of the buzzing city as tapas bars and art museums. But Pedralbes Monastery is special. Hidden away from the modern city, the monastery preserves its heavenly feeling of peace and calm. Make a pilgrimage here and the only sounds you'll hear in the 14th-century cloisters are the bubbling of fountains and the singing of resident nuns.

MUHBA EL CALL

**Map 1; Placeta de Manuel Ribé, 3, Gothic Quarter; ///response.diner.regard;
www. barcelona.cat/museuhistoria/en/muhba-el-call**

Before the Spanish Inquisition, when Catholic monarchs sought to
convert those of other faiths (often by torture), a thriving Jewish
community lived in a patch of the Gothic Quarter (called El Call).
This dimly lit 13th-century house gives a fascinating insight into their
lives and lasting influence on the city.

EL BORN CENTRE DE
CULTURA I MEMÒRIA

**Map 1; Plaça Comercia,l 12, Born; ///upcoming.puppy.talents;
www.elbornculturaimemoria.barcelona.cat**

Parents trying to instil some Catalan spirit in their kids are regulars
at this cultural centre in Born. We say centre, it's more of an
archaeological site. In 1994, renovation of a market building was
put on hold when ruins of the old city emerged. Today, information
boards tell the story of the 1713–1714 War of Succession, in which

Under Franco, the prison Carcel
La Model was crowded with
political prisoners and anti-
fascists. Remember this injustice
by paying a visit; tours are in
Catalan and Spanish but English
tours are said to be coming
(*www.lamodel.barcelona*).

Barcelona fell to the French and Spanish and this area of the city was razed to the ground. It was then, too, that the Catalan language was banned, and not for the last time: Franco would do the same some 200 years later.

» **Don't leave without** stopping by Santa Maria del Mar, a rare church built by the city's tradespeople rather than the aristocracy.

GAUDÍ HOUSE MUSEUM

Map 6; Carretera del Carmel, 23, Gràcia; ///divides.sharp.desktop;
www.casamuseugaudi.org

Barcelona's architectural heritage runs deep; just look up to see the whimsical *Modernista* style that boomed in the late 19th century. The poster boy for this ground-breaking movement was none other than local boy Antoni Gaudí. Mega fans make for this museum, which was once the architect's house.

MUSEUM OF THE OLYMPICS & SPORT AND OLYMPIC STADIUM

Map 3; Avinguda de l'Estadi, 60, Montjuïc; ///wizards.topping.tall;
www.museuolimpicbcn.cat

It was the 1992 Olympics that put Barcelona firmly on the tourist map. Take a deep dive into all this and more at the Museum of the Olympics & Sport before crossing over the road to enter the stadium where the 1992 magic took place. Interesting fact: the stadium was built in 1936 – not in the 1990s – as an anti-fascist protest against the Berlin Olympics.

Modernista Barcelona

Don't be fooled by the word Modernista; Barna's defining architectural style is flouncier than its austere Modernist counterparts. The much-loved Sagrada Família is justifiably famous but other gems lie in wait.

ELS QUATRE GATS

Map 1; Carrer de Montsió 3, Gothic Quarter; ///miracle.slices.herb; www.4gats.com

Say *hola* to Barcelona's answer to Le Chat Noir in Paris (Els Quatre Gats means "The Four Cats"). This delightful bar was the meeting place for *Modernistes and* creative thinkers in the early 20th century (Picasso held his first exhibition here). Our top tip? Come by in the evening for live piano music with fellow sophisticates.

QUADRAT D'OR

Map 4; Quadrat d'Or, Eixample; ///closet.thudded.truth

Stretching from Carrer d'Aribau to Passeig de Sant Joan, "Golden Square" is home to the greatest concentration of *Modernista* buildings in Barcelona. Look up as you *passejar* (stroll through) and you'll notice neo-Gothic features, stained-glass and intricate details that define the works of Gaudí and his contemporaries. And if you need a paracetamol after a heavy night in the bars of Raval, many of the quadrant's pharmacies are unexpectedly decadent examples of Catalan *Modernisme* (Farmàcia Aguilar Pérez is especially lovely).

PALAU DE LA MÚSICA CATALANA
Map 1; Carrer del Palau de la Música 4–6, Born; ///chew.tested.beefed; www.palaumusica.cat

Parents in town? The darling of Barcelona's *Modernista* scene is just the ticket. Designed by Barcelona-born Lluís Domènech i Montaner, this music hall was built for the Catalan Choral Society. Today you don't have to be a classical music buff to enjoy the space; concerts cover jazz, flamenco and even pop. That aside, the real star of the show is the breathtaking inverted stained-glass dome ceiling.

HOSPITAL DE LA SANTA CREU I SANT PAU
Map 6; Carrer de Sant Antoni Maria Claret 167, El Guinardó; ///twinge.retiring.paints; www.santpaubarcelona.org

Another masterpiece by Domènech i Montaner, this gorgeous hospital was converted into a museum in 2009. Make a morning of it: digest some architectural and medical history, then sit and soak up the sun – nature's best medicine – among the orange trees.

» Don't leave without exiting the hospital grounds via Avinguda Gaudí and following the road all the way to the Sagrada Família.

Solo, Pair, Crowd

A day in Barcelona without a slice
of *Modernisme* is unthinkable.
Whoever you're with, here are a
few ways to get a fix.

FLYING SOLO
Working 9 to 5
In Barcelona for business? Book a desk at
Casa de les Punxes, a grand *Modernista*
house that's now a co-working space with
an all-important café. It beats the office.

IN A PAIR
Let the music play
Slip on your Sunday best and treat yourself
and a loved one to a swanky performance
at Palau de la Música Catalana. An after-
show glass of cava in the foyer bar is a must.

FOR A CROWD
Party in the park
Stock up on picnic goodies from
Mercat de Lesseps and make for Parc
Güell. With bizarre architecture and
glorious gardens, you and your pals are
guaranteed a striking spot.

CASA AMATLLER

**Map 4; Passeig de Gràcia 41, Eixample; ///arrives.coaster.softest;
www.amatller.org**

Often playing second (or third) fiddle to Gaudí's Casa Batlló and
Casa Milà, this Gothic-inspired gem is wonderfully playful in style.
Marvel at its grandeur and decorative flourishes before heading to
the on-site hot chocolate café; Josep Puig i Cadafalch designed the
house for Barcelona's biggest chocolate magnate.

BELLESGUARD

**Map 6; Carrer de Bellesguard 20, Sant Gervasi;
///together.report.brochure; www.bellesguardgaudi.com**

While tourists flock to *Modernista* big-hitters, those seeking a
moment of reflection head to this lovely Gaudí manor house.
Tucked away on the city limits, the gardens are dotted with the
remains of a medieval castle that Gaudí took inspiration from.
» Don't leave without taking a look around CosmoCaixa while you're
here. The science museum is housed in a red-brick *Modernista* factory.

PALAU GÜELL

**Map 2; Carrer Nou de la Rambla 3–5, Raval; ///spark.driveway.small;
www.palauguell.cat**

Many have absent-mindedly strolled past this mansion, which isn't
much to look at from the outside. And yet Palau Güell is considered
one of Gaudí's best designs. You need to step inside to see why (look
to the stained-glass windows casting colours across the dark stone).

Art Museums

Picasso, Dalí, Miró – these giants of the art world all once called Barcelona home. The city is still pumping out artists to this day, and its institutions continue to mount masterpieces for the public to swoon over.

MACBA

Map 2; Plaça dels Àngels, 1, Raval; ///cutaway.unrealistic.frost; www.macba.cat

Crowds of beer-swigging skaters and gutterpunks loitering out front, rap battles filling the air on the patio to the side; there's little doubt that MACBA is one of Barcelona's edgier museums. This place is not about pretty paintings of flowers. No: here, the ever-changing exhibits draw the young and curious with topics ranging from architecture to zines, all with a focus on contemporary social issues.

MUSEU PICASSO

Map 1; Carrer de Montcada, 15–23, Born; ///deluded.trumped.tamed; www.museupicasso.bcn.cat

All of the famous Picasso works that you're hoping to see are in museums in other Spanish cities. But it doesn't matter. Here in Barcelona – the artist's one-time home – fans can take a deep

The Picasso Museum is free of charge on Thursday afternoons after 4pm and the MNAC on Saturdays.

dive into some of his lesser-known creations (we're talking pottery, sketches, metalwork) in one of the most extensive Picasso collections in the world.

MNAC

Map 3; entrance via Avinguda dels Montanyans, Montjuïc;
///sticking.strict.nation; www.museunacional.cat

Let's be honest, contemporary art isn't for everyone. For those who prefer things a little more traditional, the Museu Nacional d'Art de Catalunya (MNAC to its friends) is a great one-stop-shop for all things Catalan art-related. The main event is the Romanesque section, which features gorgeous chapels pulled from early Medieval churches in the Pyrenees.

» Don't leave without wandering round the back to find the Jardí Botànic Històric, a shady botanical garden built in a disused quarry.

DISSENY HUB

Map 5; Plaça de les Glòries Catalanes, 38, Poblenou;
///diplomat.factories.dolphin; www.ajuntament.barcelona.cat/dissenyhub

Yes, Barcelona has a long history with architecture and the decorative arts but it's not all about fancy houses and ceramic bowls. The Disseny Hub (or "Design Hub") takes visitors on a journey through all aspects of design: propaganda posters, household appliances, fashion. It's diverse and all-encompassing – there's even some design love for the humdrum toilet.

LA VIRREINA CENTRE DE LA IMATGE
Map 2; La Rambla, 99, Raval; ///best.frowns.winks;
www.ajuntament.barcelona.cat/lavirreina

Just off the thronging tourist trap of La Rambla lies this space
dedicated to all things photography. Thought-provoking, modern
and (wonderfully) free, exhibitions are constantly changing. Previous
displays include retrospectives of artists Sophie Calle and Paula Rego;
a look at society via portraits of Barcelonans taken across 30 years;
and explorations of events in recent history, such as the Arab Spring.

FUNDACIÓ TÀPIES
Map 4; Carrer d'Aragó, 255, Eixample; ///unwell.rainy.fizzle;
www.fundaciotapies.org

Meet local lad Antoni Tàpies, one of Catalunya's most experimental
artists of the postwar period. (Don't worry if you've never heard of
him, even some locals haven't.) Largely self-taught, he created heavily
textured works that were frequently inspired by Catalan culture and
language. If you're a fan of all things avant-garde or are just up for
something different, it's well worth checking out the rotating exhibitions.

MOCO MUSEUM
Map 1; Carrer de Montcada, 25, Born; ///running.cool.career;
www.mocomuseum.com

Situated in a 16th-century palace once reserved for the elite,
fresh-faced Moco (it opened in 2021) is the city's most photogenic
gallery, inside and out. The walls are hung with an abundance of

contemporary artworks, by the likes of Warhol, Basquiat, Banksy and Dalí. Newer works include Moco's immersive digital installations – such as Studio Irma's *Diamond Matrix*, a Kusama-esque room of mirrors and lights – that will be the envy of all your social media followers.

CAIXAFORUM

Map 3; Avinguda de Francesc Ferrer i Guàrdia, 6–8, Montjuïc; ///treaties.rocks.trains; www.caixaforum.es

By day, families flock to this red-brick *Modernista* factory for a dose of culture; exhibitions here touch on everything from ancient artifacts to video game art, and all have educational spaces to keep little ones engaged. Come evening, the grown-ups take over, enjoying talks, concerts and film screenings in the entrance hall.

FUNDACIÓ JOAN MIRÓ

Map 3; entrance via Avinguda Miramar, Montjuïc; ///prompting.panning.deliver; www.fmirobcn.org

Art buffs and students alike come to worship at this shrine to Barcelona-born Joan Miró, Catalunya's most famous Surrealist painter and sculptor. The striking concrete museum – a gem in its own right, architecturally speaking – is a great place to get up close and personal with the artist's work, which showcases his bold use of colour and experimental shapes.

» Don't leave without taking a stroll to Parc Joan Miró to see the 22-m- (72-ft-) high Miró sculpture *Dona i Ocell*.

Cultural Spaces

Yes, Gaudí and Picasso were talented but culture in Barcelona doesn't stop with them. The city has countless spaces that celebrate cinema, performance art and LGBTQ+ stories. Oh, and puppets.

LA CASA DELS ENTREMESOS

Map 1; Plaça de les Beates, 2, Born; ///testers.drill.referral;
www.lacasadelsentremesos.cat

We know, a space dedicated to giant puppets seems odd but *els gegants* are (literally) big in Catalan culture. These 4-m- (13-ft)- tall puppets dance with revellers during the *festes majors* (*barri* festivals usually celebrated in the summer months). Each *barri* has its own pair, some of them centuries old. When the party's over, these curious figures of local folklore are housed at La Casa dels Entremesos.

IDEAL

Map 5; Carrer del Dr Trueta 196, Poblenou; ///helpless.brittle.yarn;
www.idealbarcelona.com

Once a cinema, then a TV studio and now a temple to the digital arts, IDEAL is all about immersing visitors in its temporary and truly one-of-a-kind displays. Poblenou's creatives spend hours taking in the centre's wall-to-wall holograms, which celebrate the works of specific artists, such as Gustav Klimt or Frida Kahlo. Elements of the masters' works are projected onto the walls of the centre's vast rooms, immersing goggle-eyed spectators into larger-than-life versions of iconic paintings.

CCCB

Map 2; Carrer de Montalegre 5, Raval; ///answers.singer.booth; www.cccb.org

Ravers raise the roof at the Centre de Cultura Contemporània (CCCB) during the summer months, when the contemporary arts centre hosts performances for Sónar and Primavera Sound music festivals. The rest of the year, this is where the curious-minded get a dose of culture by enjoying exhibitions on everything from bacteria to Björk, and attending talks on things like the power and politics of a face mask.

» Don't leave without making the most of the CCCB's ultra-modern VR experiences. Advance booking is an absolute must.

Try it!
STREET ART TOUR

Murals are tagged and updated every day in Barna. Join the good folk of Street Art Barcelona on a tour to find the art in Raval, Born and Poblenou on that given day (www.streetartbcn.com).

CENTRE LGBTI

Map 3; Carrer del Comte Borrell, 22, Sant Antoni;
///shopper.passages.secondly; www.ajuntament.barcelona.cat/lgtbi

In a place where being yourself is celebrated, a city council-run centre that's all about honouring queer culture just makes sense. Art installations and photography exhibitions are small but they pack a punch, spotlighting LGBTQ+ stories from a range of perspectives. It's a great spot to mingle with the community without having to fork out at a bar or shout over a deafening sound system.

ARTS SANTA MÒNICA

Map 2; La Rambla, 7, Raval; ///washed.defends.clubs;
https://artssantamonica.gencat.cat

This building might once have been a Renaissance convent but nothing is sacred here, not since Arts Santa Mònica was set up as an interdisciplinary arts centre in the 1980s. The space is a platform for

Visual arts centre Hangar, in Poblenou, supports young artists and writers by giving them space to create within its walls *(www.hangar.org)*. Little do many locals realize that on Thursdays the centre opens its doors so that the general public can watch the young hopefuls hard at work. Who knows, in a few months' time you might see their work on display or staged at Arts Santa Mònica.

young, up-and-coming artists with a different take on things. Collective projects blur the lines between art practices, with concerts staging medieval compositions in the style of pop queen Madonna, and performances of feminist texts given through the medium of dance.

» **Don't leave without** having a drink at the bar lounge, where the centre's podcast is recorded – you might even be approached to feature.

FILMOTECA DE CATALUNYA
Map 2; Plaça de Salvador Seguí, 1, Raval; ///races.juggler.rankings; www.filmoteca.cat

Cinephiles come together at this film archive and cinema, one of the few spots in the city where you can watch films in their original language (Spain dubs almost everything, unfortunately). Film-themed artifacts are laid out in the centre's exhibition rooms, while two screens showcase indie, foreign and classic flicks.

BIBLIOTECA PUBLICA ARÚS
Map 5; Passeig de Sant Joan, 26, Eixample; ///rail.hails.glides; www.bpa.es

Okay, this one isn't technically a cultural space per se, but it's too beautiful to miss. The legacy of Catalan journalist and playwright Rossend Arús, this gorgeous library houses one of the largest collections of books on Freemasonry in the world. Arús hosted Freemason meetings here in the late 1800s before he left the building and his collection of books to the people of Barcelona. You can't take books out bu you're here to take in the sumptuous grandeur.

Get Crafty

Design-savvy Barcelona is a city of makers, and locals love crafting their own little something to take home. Follow their lead and set your creative juices flowing at these varied crafty experiences.

ART&WINE

Map 4; Carrer de la Mare de Déu dels Desemparats 14, Gràcia; ///staging.spelled.goggles; www.artwine.es

Feeling creatively blocked? Always been scared of picking up a paintbrush and letting your imagination run free? There's one simple solution: wine. Art&Wine runs sessions every evening with professional art teachers, to help you bring out your artistic side and give you a chance to socialize with other creatives, all in the most Barcelonan way possible – over a drink.

KANAY TALLER DE CERÀMICA

Map 5; Carrer del Bruc 5, Born; ///preoccupied.struts.promises; www.studiokanay.com

Ceramics are huge in Barna; pick out any group of 30-somethings and you can guarantee one of them attends a ceramics class. Kanay offers a range of workshops, from one-day courses to mastering the potter's wheel. If you don't feel like doing a Demi Moore and getting your hands all covered in clay, sign-up for a short pottery painting workshop instead.

BARCELONA WOOD WORKSHOPS
Map 6; Carrer del Pacífic 29, Sant Andreu; ///surprise.immunity.desire; www.barcelonawoodworkshops.com

Founded by architect and craftswoman extraordinaire Andrea Cortés, Barcelona Wood Workshops brings together Andrea's two main passions: woodwork and sharing her craft with others. Alongside her team of fellow woodworkers, Andrea runs various workshops, from carving spoons to creating a traditional *cajón* (a box-shaped drum used in flamenco). Good luck trying to cram the latter into your suitcase.

» Don't leave without calling at nearby Nau Bostik, a former factory now home to many creative businesses and regular vintage markets.

TALLER DE 4 PINTORS
Map 1; Carrer de la Portaferrissa 16, Gothic Quarter; ///fattest.reboot.tape; www.tallerde4pintors.cat

What could be more bohemian than a painting and drawing workshop overlooking the spires of the Gothic Quarter? Run by two professional artists, Nuria and Agustí, these classes will help you hone your art skills whether you're just there for a one-off or you've signed up for a series of lessons. With so much inspiration on hand, it's almost impossible not to improve.

CERAMIC ART STUDIO 137°

**Map 5; Carrer de Llull 256, Poblenou; ///dream.boldest.poem;
www.137degrees.com**

Poblenou is one of the most creative neighbourhoods in Barcelona, so it follows that its local pottery studio offers some of the city's most interesting courses. Try your hand at a fun new challenge, like abstract sculpture or making your own ceramic sushi set.

» Don't leave without strolling over to Espai Joliu *(p70)* for a top-notch coffee and plenty of design magazines to peruse for inspiration.

THE ESPADRILLES EXPERIENCE

**Map 1; Carrer de la Llibreteria 9, Gothic Quarter;
///luggage.faces.bared; www.espadrillesexperience.com**

Love them or loathe them, *espardenyes* (or espadrilles) are cool for the summer and rooted in Catalan folk culture. Dating back to the 14th century, these shoes were worn by the working classes who could afford the *esparto* grass needed to make them. Luis and Kathe at Handmade Barcelona share this heritage at their workshops.

ATUELL CERÀMICA

**Map 4; Carrer del Montseny 45, Gràcia; ///faced.stacks.layered;
www.atuell.com**

Did we mention that Barcelonans are massively into their pottery classes? Well Atuell is where they hone their new-found skills. This open workshop comes with wheels and kilns, plus a team on hand to help with any questions. It's perfect if you're already handy with your clay.

Liked by the locals

"When you make your own pair of espadrilles at Handmade, you become part of the community of artisans of Barcelona. Every time you wear a pair of shoes that you've made yourself, you remember your trip even more vividly. That's the magic of this experience."

LUIS MORENO, FOUNDER OF HANDMADE BARCELONA
AND THE ESPADRILLES EXPERIENCE

A day of
Civil War history

A bloody war played out in Barcelona's streets less than 100 years ago. From 1936 to 1939, right-wing Nationalists led by Franco rained bombs on the city, bringing Barcelona (and wider Catalunya) to its knees. Decades of Catalan oppression ensued under Franco's regime, ending with his death in 1975. The scars of this dark history continue to shape the region's political landscape today.

1. Palau de la Generalitat de Catalunya
Plaça de Sant Jaume, Gothic Quarter
///transfers.fish.whom

2. Plaça de Sant Felip Neri
Gothic Quarter
///squeezed.scout.swept

3. Caelum
Carrer de la Palla, 8; Gothic Quarter; 933 026 993
///levels.teaspoons.migrate

4. Hotel Continental
La Rambla, 138, Eixample;
www.hotelcontinental.com
///sports.exposing.tolls

5. Plaça de Catalunya
Eixample
///parrot.theme.reshape

6. La Rosa de Foc
Carrer de Joaquín Costa, 34, Raval; 933 177 892
///others.brands.huddle

7. Bar Marsella
Carrer de Sant Pau, 65, Raval
///recoup.gold.warm

Apple store ///ranges.typical.door

**Pop into
LA ROSA DE FOC**
Buy a thought-provoking read from this politically minded bookshop, which is run by a trade union.

CARRER DELS TALLE

GRAN VIA DE LES CORTS CATALANES

PLAÇA D ÀNGE

CARRER DE JOAQUÍ

CARRER DE LA RIERA ALTA

PLAÇA DEL PEDRÓ

In 1939, banners of Lenin and Stalin hung across the facade of the Communist Party HQ, a building that now houses the **Apple store**.

PLAÇA DE CATALUNYA

PLAÇA DE LLUIS MILLET

CARRER DE SANT PERE MÉS ALT

AV. DE FRANCESC CAMBO

VIA LAIETANA

Pause in
PLAÇA DE CATALUNYA
5

nire the monument
Catalan nationalist
:esc Macià i Llussa.
nbolizes the causes
he politician fought
for: republicanism
and socialism.

4

Give a nod to the
HOTEL CONTINENTAL

Pass the hotel where George Orwell wrote *Homage to Catalonia*; it was here that he nursed wounds he'd amassed while fighting for the Republic.

Walk through
PLAÇA DE SANT FELIP NERI

The buildings surrounding this square are pockmarked with shrapnel holes, remnants of an Italian bombardment, in 1938, that killed 42 people.

CARRER D'ELISABETS

LA RAMBLA

CARRER DE LA PORTAFERRISSA

CARRER DEL PI

CARRER DE LA PORTAFERRISSA

2

3

CARRER DE ST. HONORAT

1

CARRER DE JAUME I

Enjoy a sweet treat at
CAELUM

Take a break at Caelum (Latin for "heaven"). Everything here is baked by Spanish monks and nuns.

GOTHIC QUARTER

Start your journey at
PALAU DE LA GENERALITAT DE CATALUNYA

Take in the offices of the Catalan Government, the institution of which was abolished under Franco in 1940. An underground air raid shelter was unearthed here a few years ago.

CARRER DEL CARME

CARRER DE L'HOSPITAL

CARRER DE FERRAN

RAVAL

CARRER DE

LA RAMBLA

PLAÇA REIAL

Finish up at
BAR MARSELLA

You've earned a drink. Reflect on your day at Bar Marsella, where Civil War correspondent Ernest Hemingway spent many an evening.

RAMBLA DEL RAVAL

7

| 0 metres | 200 |
| 0 yards | 200 |

NIGHTLIFE

Life doesn't stop when the sun goes down in Barna – if anything, it just gets started. Nights pass hopping between sultry terraces, legendary queer bars and revelrous clubs.

LGBTQ+ Scene

On paper, Spain is one of the most Catholic countries in Europe – and it's also one of the most LGBTQ+-friendly. However you identify, Barcelona will welcome you with open arms.

LA CHAPELLE

Map 4; Carrer de Muntaner, 67, Eixample; ///closed.bluntly.acting; 934 533 076

Nowhere embodies Spain's contradiction of Catholic and queer better than La Chapelle. Decked out with more Catholic iconography than you can shake a crosier at, the Eixample club could have been the setting of Madonna's *Like a Prayer* video. Be sure to arrive early to get in (by early, we mean 10pm).

SAFARI DISCO CLUB

Map 3; Carrer de Tarragona, 141, Sants; ///burns.migrants.leave; www.safaridiscoclub.com

A lot of clubs were victims of the pandemic but LGBTQ+ stronghold Safari Disco Club is still standing. Come the weekend, this is where Barna's queer community head for reliable club nights, dancing their troubles away to reggaeton, house and, of course, classic club hits.

CANDY DARLING

**Map 4; Gran Via de les Corts Catalanes, 586, Sant Antoni;
///honestly.safe.mouse; www.candydarlingbcn.com**

You know a bar is well versed in its queer history when pink triangles
– once a Nazi badge of shame – are reclaimed to signal LGBTQ+
pride. Named after American trans icon Candy Darling, this unusually
roomy (for Barna) bar is the place of choice for out-and-proud locals.
Expect a line-up of experimental queer artists and plenty of voguing.

CARITA BONITA

**Map 4; Carrer de Balmes, 69, Eixample; ///thunder.teaches.tonight;
685 999 635**

Split into different areas, Barcelona's lesbian bar *par excellence* is
whatever you need it to be. Looking to catch up with a friend over a
mojito? There's a laid-back space for that. You and the gang planning
to dance the night away? Carita Bonita's dance floor won't disappoint.
>> Don't leave without chatting to the bar staff – Carita Bonita has
some of the friendliest in the city.

EL CANGREJO

Map 2; Carrer de Montserrat 9, Raval; ///active.grades.acrobat; 933 012 978

Nights out don't get more in-your-face than at this bastion of queer
culture. Like their sisters who performed here in the 1990s, drag acts
draw heavily on local pop culture and flamenco, and are obsessed
with Spanish divas. They love a lewd joke, too, and will pull audience
members up on stage. You've been warned.

MADAME JASMINE

Map 2; Rambla del Raval, 22, Raval; ///boarding.custard.gives

Tiger-print fur on the wall, fringed lamps hanging from the ceiling and bartenders wrapped in capes and shawls: Madame Jasmine is the underground of local drag. This deliciously debauched bar is the go-to for Barcelona's rag-tag crowd of gutterpunks, who take advantage of the communal pots of glitter and rhinestones to get themselves looking the part, all while sipping potent cocktails.

» Don't leave without visiting the toilet to read printouts of the bar's (few) bad online reviews lining the bathroom walls.

LA FEDERICA

Map 3; Carrer de Salvà 3, Poble Sec; ///humans.gearing.relax; 936 005 901

Looking for something a bit more chilled? Seventies-themed La Federica is the best spot to nurse a beer in the company of a laid-back crowd. Chat to the bar staff about the bar's latest art exhibition (most artworks on the walls are for sale) or swing by for a charity drag bingo night (just make sure you can count from *uno* to *cien*).

BELIEVE CLUB

Map 4; Carrer de Balmes 56, Eixample; ///glitter.palaces.darkest; www.thebelieve.club

Things get going around midnight at Barcelona's drag cabaret and continue into the early hours. Sure, this LGBTQ+ club doesn't break the mould with its choice of music, but on those nights when you just need a beer and a dance, Believe delivers.

Liked by the locals

"Barcelona's drag and queer scene has a huge range of options – from Believe, where you'll see the next generation of drag acts, to Ocaña, where the city's living legends perform. But if you want to discover real Barcelona, head to Madame Jasmine for the underground queer scene."

TONI SOBRINO/VILMA PROUX, DRAG ARTIST

Cool Clubs

*Ask any southern European and they'll tell you that Barna is **the** place to go clubbing. Be sure to have an afternoon siesta before a big night out, mind; the party really gets going around 3am, after all.*

APOLO

Map 3; Carrer Nou de la Rambla, 113, Poble Sec;
///pipeline.respond.bundles; www.sala-apolo.com

If Barcelona is a clubbing capital, then Apolo is its royal palace. Once upon a time this grand ballroom was the crowning glory of the theatre scene around Avinguda del Paral·lel. Now discerning Barcelonans dance under its chandeliers to the beats of the most prestigious names in dance music at weekend club nights.

RAZZMATAZZ

Map 5; Carrer dels Almogàvers, 122, Poblenou; ///exact.cookery.pancake;
www.salarazzmatazz.com

We know, we know, a club in an old factory is nothing new but the scale of Razzmatazz is truly something to behold. With all the grimy-chic trimmings you'd expect of a post-industrial setting, this heavy-weight has five party rooms (six if you count the toilet where DJ sets sometimes take place), each with its own personality. Razz Club is all about pop and indie classics; the Loft is the favourite for house and techno; Popbar is the de facto queer space; Lolita plays Italo-disco and funk; and Trill is for everything urban (think grime and reggaeton).

» **Don't leave without** hanging around on the terraces that link the rooms at Razzmatazz; it's the best place to make friends, especially if you have a cigarette to give away.

MOOG

Map 2; Carrer de l'Arc del Teatre, 3, Raval; ///eating.ranking.attend; www.moogbarcelona.com

It might be the size of a postage stamp but there's always enough space at Moog. Two-step on inside and you'll first be met by hardcore ravers headbanging to techno blaring from one of the best sound systems in the city. Continue upstairs where a hall of mirrors forms the stage for resident DJ Purpur, who plays favourite 80s and 90s hits while doing Beyoncé-style hairography in front of a fan.

BUS TERRAZA

Map 6; Avinguda del Litoral, 488, Diagonal Mar i Forum; ///thumps.danger.coupler; www.busterraza.com

Not a night owl but still like a party? This is your place. Order a *jarra de sangría* to share with your troupe in the early afternoon and let the volume and techno rhythm carry you away into the night. When you start to feel peckish, the club's London-style bus is on hand with *bikinis* (Catalan sandwiches) – perfect fuel for a few more hours of partying.

LA TERRRAZZA

Map 3; Avinguda Francesc Ferrer i Guàrdia s/n, Montjuïc;
///hedge.leaflet.waddle; www.laterrrazza.com

What could be more magical than dancing the night away under the stars? We know: dancing under the stars at a replica 16th-century farmhouse surrounded by palm trees. Yes, La Terrrazza might be awash with international crowds rather than born-and-bred Barcelonans, making the drink prices a little higher than at other clubs. But the setting!

SIDECAR

Map 1; Plaça Reial, 7, Gothic Quarter; ///minder.pepper.outings;
www.sidecar.es

Barna's club scene errs towards electro but, indie fans, fear not: there's refuge for you in the form of Sidecar. Descend the stairs by the entrance on Plaça Reial and you'll find yourself in a sweltering basement where 30-somethings nod to their favourite rock anthems.

» Don't leave without checking out upcoming concerts for some real-life, in-your-face rock, rap and indie music.

MARULA CAFÉ

Map 1; Carrer dels Escudellers, 49, Gothic Quarter;
///earliest.smoking.refuse; www.marulacafe.com

Velvet bar-stools, rich red curtains and a disco ball hanging from the ceiling: retro Marula Café is one classy joint. The music is just as elegant, with an owner of Barcelona City Records *(p100)* frequently

Marula Café is very popular with Barcelonans so get here around 1am to secure your patch.

starring as DJ. He spins disco, funk, afrobeat and soul records on vinyl – *always* on vinyl – to an appreciative crowd of music connoisseurs.

LAUT

Map 3; Carrer de Vila i Vilà, 63, Poble Sec; ///organs.communal.pilots; www.laut.es

The best things in life come in small packages. Take Laut, a little avant-garde club that punches above its weight thanks to its killer sound system (hinted at in its name; *laut* means "loud" in German). After a hard week at work, the city's coolest lace up their favourite trainers and make for a night out here, safe in the knowledge that Laut will deliver a carefully curated experimental programme of up-and-coming names on the electronic scene.

MACARENA CLUB

Map 1; Carrer Nou de Sant Francesc, 5, Gothic Quarter; ///goals.slippery.design; www.macarenaclub.com

First things first, you're not going to be dancing the Macarena here, despite the club's name. That is unless you can make your aunt's favourite dance moves match some of the hardest hitting house and techno baselines in the city (doubtful). Macarena Club is unusually convivial for a hardcore techno club (not to mention very small) so you'll likely find yourself making new friends as you live your best life on the dance floor.

Late-Night Bars

Big night out ahead? Fancy one more drink before bed? Barna has loads of late-night bars where locals keep the party going, which – given that clubbing doesn't really get going until late – is a godsend.

NEVERMIND

Map 2; Carrer dels Tallers, 68, Raval; ///herds.release.status; 663 710 095

Ever feel the urge to ditch your drink for your board? Barcelonans sure do – skating is a big deal here in Barna – and Nevermind is on hand for those moments. This gritty spot in Raval is a skater's

Hidden away down a tiny alleyway in uber-trendy Gràcia lies Musical Maria *(Carrer de Maria, 5)*. Can't spot it? Look for the omnipresent crowd of smokers hanging around the door. The dive bar is a literal temple to rock music (don't expect any club hits here), its walls covered in shrine-like music memorabilia. Make yourself at home with the motley crew of punters, all swigging beer and swapping life stories across the stained pool table.

paradise, with its indoor half-pipe, graffiti-splattered walls and soundtrack of crunchy grunge. Not a skateboarder? Fear not. Skaters are only too happy to provide some late-night entertainment while you kick-back with a (dirt-cheap) beer.

OCAÑA

Map 1; Plaça Reial, 13–15, Gothic Quarter; ///invite.printers.hiking; www.ocana.cat

When the locals are feeling fancy and want to flaunt it, LGBTQ+ bar Ocaña is where they go. Those looking for a sedate drink settle in on the decadent ground floor, which is all stylish candelabras and exposed beams. Beneath their feet, things are much more lively in the basement (aren't they always?) thanks to DJ sets and live performances. With cocktails flowing and plenty of space to dance, even those upstairs are tempted below deck to let out their wilder side.

FOXY BAR

Map 2; Carrer de la Riera Alta, 59, Raval; ///popping.dishes.paves; 935 017 465

Foxy might look like your grandma's living room, with its vintage flock wallpaper and chintzy furniture, but Raval locals know it as a vibey bar – just the job for a date. Order a couple of mojitos, recline on plush chaise longes and while away what remains of the night trying to decipher the quirky paraphernalia hanging from the walls.

» Don't leave without stopping in at Els Tres Tombs, around the corner. It's a great place to people-watch Barcelona's night owls.

GUZZO CLUB

Map 1; Plaça Comercial, 10, Born; ///clocks.harvest.pound;
www.guzzorestaurante.es

Early evening is dinnertime at Guzzo Club but as midnight ticks closer the place transforms into a late-night party. Diners get tipsy on creative cocktails, and cool kids turn up for the live jazz acts. The whole place has a wonderfully artsy feel, with upcycled furniture and graffiti-covered walls (often painted to a live audience).

» Don't leave without having a bite here; the dishes are truly gourmet and beautifully presented.

CURTIS AUDIOPHILE CAFÉ

Map 4; Carrer de Mallorca, 196, Eixample; ///unusually.fended.gross;
www.curtisaudiocafe.com

It's all about the sanctity of music at this late-night café. Top-notch speakers surround the bar, DJs perform curated sets and boxes of records wait to be rummaged through. Order a vermouth and make use of the vinyl listening stations.

POLAROID BAR

Map 1; Carrer dels Còdols, 29, Gothic Quarter; ///tenses.juniors.prop;
www.polaroidbar.es

Hop into your DeLorean or, failing that, hail a taxi: we're going back to the 80s. Sure, the Space Invaders murals, ET bike hanging from the ceiling and VHS tapes plastered across the walls are bordering on tacky, but what's wrong with that? If you need help getting into

Want more retro shenanigans? Turn up on a Sunday night for hotdogs and cult movie screenings.

the mood, take a look at Polaroid's menu of kitsch cocktails – perhaps try a *Flashdance* with cachaça and passionfruit or a fittingly red, vodka-based *Beetlejuice*.

MANCHESTER

Map 1; Carrer de Milans, 5, Gothic Quarter; ///gushes.camps.judge; www.manchesterbar.com

Yes, this one is a bit of a dive: the walls are plastered with ageing band memorabilia, sticky tables pepper the place and the smell of spilled beer lingers (at a euro a pop, people aren't so careful with their drinks). But that's all part of the charm. Paying homage to Britain's music-making city of Manchester, this buzzy bar is the last stop of the night for die-hard indie fans and Anglophiles. Together they bop down memory lane to the soundtrack of Joy Division, The Smiths and The Stone Roses.

33/45

Map 2; Carrer de Joaquín Costa, 4, Raval; ///averts.passes.gloves; www.3345.es

After-hours drinks don't have to be raucous. Take this low-key spot, where scenesters break up the night before hitting the next bar. They sink gratefully into the bar's leather armchairs and sofas (no booze-soaked barrels to crane over or wonky stools to teeter on here), sip 33/45's famous tequila cocktails and gaze dreamily at the for-sale artworks dotted across the walls.

Live Music

People from all walks of life gather in Barcelona's live music venues, all looking to be carried away by the music. And with everything from jazz to flamenco, there's a show for every night of the week.

CENTRE CULTURAL ALBAREDA

Map 3; Carrer d'Albareda, 22, Poble Sec; ///change.bared.stags; www.ajuntament.barcelona.cat/ccivics/albareda

Poble Sec locals count themselves lucky to have this gem on their doorstep and we see why. One of several city council-run centres promoting culture in all its forms, Albareda specializes in music and offers a platform to unknown acts. Performances include things like improvised jam sessions, local youth orchestras, Caribbean-influenced hip-hop and live flamenco.

L'AUDITORI

Map 5; Carrer de Lepant 150, Glòries; ///terminal.erupts.record; www.auditori.cat

While Palau de la Música Catalana *(p121)* hogs the limelight, L'Auditori humbly goes about its business, offering the best acoustics in the city, whatever the genre. Yes, the modern music hall isn't as pretty as its

Modernista cousin, but the overshadowed spot is all about delivering what the people deserve: world-class music. Classical music is the main player, but pop, rock, folk and electronica concerts also appear on L'Auditori's first-class music programme.

» **Don't leave without** making a stop at the Museu de la Música inside L'Auditori to learn about all things music history.

HELIOGÀBAL
Map 4; Carrer de Ramón y Cajal, 80, Gràcia; ///spits.pursuit.solo; www.heliogabal.com

At this music bar, up-and-coming acts are known to lay down tunes before they make it big. Pop in for a beer with Barcelona's die-hard music lovers on the lookout for their new favourite band. Who knows? In a few years' time you might spot some familiar faces on the main stage of Primavera Sound.

Let's keep this between us, *sí*? For some truly local music, make 23 Robadors a port of call *(www.23robadors. com)*. Squeeze your way into this little rock-walled cave with its low-hanging beams (tall friends, beware) for a rowdy night of jazz, live Latin sounds and flamenco; we say flamenco but we don't mean the touristy polka-dot-dress-and-castanets kind, rather the very real, very emotional kind. Pair with well-priced beers and nibbles and you've got a night to remember.

Solo, Pair, Crowd

Whether you've got a few hours to yourself or you're craving a night out with the gang, Barcelona's music scene has got you covered.

FLYING SOLO
Art and a show
When a date with yourself is long overdue, make for Museu Europa d'Art Modern in Born. Explore the museum on a Friday or Saturday before checking out the museum's little-known music programme. You'll be serenaded with blues, jazz or classical.

IN A PAIR
Spine-tingling strings
Treat a special someone to an evening of candlelit classical guitar music in the Santa Maria del Pi church in the Gothic Quarter. Goosebumps are guaranteed.

FOR A CROWD
Groove with the gang
With live music and plenty of space to dance, Quilombo in Eixample is the ideal place for a night with your besties. As it's a dive bar, the drinks are wallet-friendly so you can party guilt-free into the early hours.

JAMBOREE JAZZ

Map 1; Plaça Reial, 17, Gothic Quarter; ///inhaled.crab.loosed;
www.jamboreejazz.com

A basement setting, crumbling brick walls, moody lighting: Jamboree
would have all the trappings of a clandestine bar were it not one of
the best-loved live music joints in the city. This local legend has kept
Barna swinging since the 60s, when the likes of Bill Coleman, Kenny
Drew and Dexter Gordon graced the pocket-sized stage. A Monday
night Jamboree jam session is a rite of passage in Barcelona,
attracting seasoned listeners and fresh-faced newbies alike.

» Don't leave without heading over to tapas bar Palosanto post-jam
to wind up your evening with some drinks and sharing plates.

EL GRAN TEATRE DEL LICEU

Map 2; La Rambla, 51–59, Raval; ///molars.defining.libraries;
www.liceubarcelona.cat

For all their love of techno and electronic music, Barcelonans are
partial to a bit of Puccini, especially in their city's opera house, of
which they're hugely proud. And we can see why: the palatial
theatre has survived fires, bombings, the Civil War, COVID-19.
Speaking of, it was during the pandemic that the Liceu made
headlines by staging a concert for 2,300 house plants (all of which
were given to healthcare workers). Today, Barcelonans are grateful
to be back in the plush red chairs, watching classics like *Carmen*, *La
Bohème* and *Die Walküre*. The under-35s among you: keep an eye
out for under-35 events, when a night at the opera (for a special
price) is followed by drinks and a DJ set up on the opera house roof.

Night Terraces

Sultry summers melt into temperate winters in Barcelona. Whatever the season, locals gravitate towards outdoor terraces to spend unhurried evenings with loved ones under the stars.

BAR CENTRAL

Map 2; Carrer d'Elisabets, 6, Raval; ///smooth.enhancement.applies; www.barcentral.bar

Looking for a laid-back spot? Make a beeline for this lush, plant-filled patio bar set in the back of a bookshop. University grads and intellectuals are regulars at this terrace, once the courtyard of an abbot's palace. Draw up a chair alongside them and drink in their spirited conversations over a glass of rioja.

ANTIC TEATRE

Map 1; Carrer de Verdaguer i Callís, 12, Born; ///smoke.bucked.bubbles; www.anticteatre.com

This vibey terrace, set in the courtyard of a theatre, has become a total hit with the locals. Sure, the furniture has seen better days, but the fairy lights strung up in the trees, the cheap beers and candles on the tables more than make up for it. A word to the wise:

If the terrace is full, walk round the corner to Plaça de Sant Pere, a charming medieval square.

if you head inside to order at the bar while there's a performance on, you will be hastily told to shh (it's happened to the best of us).

CÀMPING

Map 5; Carrer de Carmen Amaya, 18, Poblenou; ///decks.fizzy.watched; www.campingcamping.org

On a balmy night, this is the place to be. Gaggles of rowdy pals congregate at this campsite-inspired (and ultra-hipster) terrace with street food pop-ups and a strict zero-waste policy. Stretched out on the communal picnic blankets, the footloose and fancy-free clink beers and compete with other drinkers to set the music on the terrace's online jukebox. Camping has never been so fun.

» Don't leave without challenging your mates – or a friendly local – to a round of ping-pong. Ask for balls and bats at the bar.

BAR CALDERS

Map 3; Carrer del Parlament, 25, Sant Antoni; ///harvest.timidly.trifle; 933 299 349

Named after a beloved Catalan author, Bar Calders is tucked away on a little side street, giving its terrace a deliciously undiscovered feel (no *guiris* in sight). Sant Antoni locals hoof it here for an evening vermouth or a signature gin and tonic, which comes in a satisfying goldfish-bowl-sized glass. Be sure to visit earlier in the evening because once regulars get a table, they're not giving it up easily.

EL JARDÍ

Map 2; Carrer de l'Hospital, 56, Raval; ///dented.richly.ship; 936 819 234

Once the courtyard of the old medieval hospital (the building of which now houses the National Library of Catalunya), the garden bar El Jardí is totally idyllic. Barcelonans escort their out-of-town friends to this charming nook, tucked away between ancient stone walls and glowing with soft, ambient lighting. Hours pass in minutes in the storied setting, with the help of chilled music and a tempting selection of tipples.

LA CASETA DEL MIGDIA

Map 3; Mirador del Migdia s/n, Montjuïc; ///forgets.hamper.openings; www.lacaseta.org

Tucked away around the back of Montjuïc, La Caseta del Migdia stands in the middle of a secluded pine grove, overlooking the sea. No bells or whistles – this humble shack on Barna's magic mountain is lit only by a handful of lanterns and the light of the moon. There's atmosphere by the barrel-load, though, with regular BBQs, rumba concerts and DJ sets. Summer is the time to visit, bearing in mind

Try it!
DANCE WITH THE STARS

Barna is big on swing – you'll likely see locals dancing in the street. Join the friendly folk at Swing Maniacs *(www.swingmaniacs. com)* for a masterclass and dance the night away at La Caseta del Migdia.

that the terrace closes a little after sunset in the colder months. Oh, and cash is essential – the shack is so remote that the card machine doesn't always work.

FAT SCHMUCK

Map 2; Plaça d'Emili Vendrell, Raval; ///clash.nitrate.doctor; www.fatschmuck.com

Searching for a date spot on a muggy night? The terrace at Fat Schmuck won't let you down. Dotted with potted plants and lit by fairy lights, this is the perfect place to swap life stories over some of the finest cocktails in the city (the tarragon-infused Aperol spritz is our favourite). Feeling peckish? Order from the bar's menu of high-end junk food (an oxymoron, we know, but it's accurate).

SALTS

Map 3; Avinguda Miramar, 31, Montjuïc; ///monument.fields.edgy; www.saltsmontjuic.com

As the sun sets over Barcelona, the city's seagull population comes to roost on the Olympic diving pools (p175). Meanwhile, above the bleachers, things are in full swing on the terrace at Salts. Like the clamouring sports fans of 30 years ago, young people pour in expectantly, chatting excitedly to their friends. They're here for one thing and one thing only: to watch the last rays of sun colour the roofs of the city as dusk falls, drink in hand. Life is good.

» Don't leave without jumping on the Montjuïc funicular railway to take you back down to the city (it's included in the price of a metro ticket).

Built in the 1990s to revitalize Raval, today **MACBA** *is known for its skaters outside. People come from all over to show what they can do.*

PLAÇA DELS ÀNGELS

CARRER DEL CARME

Chow down at
BISMILLAH KEBABISH

4

Most nights out end at Bismillah, the best of Raval's kebab shops. Sit in or get a tasty chicken wrap for the trip home.

Get your groove on at
CARNAL COCKTAIL BAR

3

Feel the Latin rhythm at Carnal, where jazz, soul, bossa nova and tangotronica keep cocktail-sipping scenesters moving.

PLAÇA DE LA GARDUNYA

CARRER DE JOAQUIN COSTA

CARRER DE LA RIERA ALTA

CARRER DE MARIA AURÈLIA CAPMANY

CARRER DE L'HOSPITAL

Like many of its neighbours, the giant iron cat **El Gat de Botero** *searched for a home for ages before finding its place in Raval.*

PLAÇA DEL PEDRÓ

RAVAL

RAMBLA DEL RAVAL

CARRER DE LA RIERETA

Live it up at
MADAME JASMINE

2

Head to Madame Jasmine where the music's loud and the outfits are louder. This bar shirks gender norms, so don't be afraid of wearing something a little risqué.

Kick off the night at
LA CASA DE LA PRADERA

1

Start with a beer at this welcoming queer bar. Order filling Mediterranean fare from the menu at Las Fernandez, just next door, and tuck in on La Casa's terrace (the bars are good pals).

CARRER DE SANTA ELENA

0 metres	100
0 yards	100

A night out in
revelrous Raval

No matter who you are, there's a space for you in Raval. Like much here, the *barri*'s name comes from somewhere else – specifically the word *rabad*, which translates as "neighbourhood" in Arabic. And the area is defined by the various communities who have come to call it home: immigrants and anarchists, outcasts and outlaws, artists and activists. Once a no-go for tourists, Raval has transformed into a thriving area that represents the heart of Barcelona's rebellious spirit. Streets are safer and cultural institutions have opened but the *barri* remains revolutionary.

1. La Casa de la Pradera
Carrer de les Carretes, 57;
625 232 755
///typist.goods.shiver

2. Madame Jasmine
Rambla del Raval, 22;
///boarding.custard.gives

3. Carnal Cocktail Bar
Carrer de Joaquín Costa, 12;
936 014 005
///sums.spider.coder

4. Bismillah Kebabish
Carrer de Joaquín Costa, 22;
934 430 184
///barman.swanky.pies

El Gat de Botero ///spits.dampen.shaky

MACBA ///cutaway.unrealistic.frost

OUTDOORS

Waves lapping the shore, lush green spaces, buzzing public squares: it's not just year-round sun that tempts locals to while away their days outdoors.

Beautiful Beaches

Whatever the season, locals gravitate towards the beach. Sure, some are overrun with tourists (and, yes, their litter) but there are hidden spots that Barcelonans love, and you'll fall for, too.

Sant Cugat del Vallès
Santa Coloma de Gramenet
Sant Andreu de la Barca
Badalona
Santa Adrià de Besòs
⊙ Platja d'Ocata
⊙ Platja de Montgat
Sant Vicenç dels Horts
⊙ Banys del Fòrum
Vallirana
⊙ Platja de la Mar Bella
BARCELONA
l'Hospitalet de Llobregat
⊙ Platja de Sant Sebastià and Platja de Sant Miquel
Torrelles de Llobregat
Villadecans
El Prat de Llobregat
Mediterranean Sea
Castelldefels
⊙ Platja del Prat
0 kilometres   10
0 miles   10
Sitges
⊙ Platja del Garraf

PLATJA DE MONTGAT

Entrance via Carrer del Mar, Montgat; ///that.milkman.rosette; www.montgat.cat

At long last, the weekend has arrived! Pack a bag and get a good night's sleep; in the morning, you're catching a train to the city's outer fringes for a day at Montgat beach. Perhaps you'll rent a dinghy and bob about on the crystal clear water, or make a start on that novel under the shade of a beach umbrella. Either way, life doesn't get much better.

» **Don't leave without** keeping yourself going with some snacks and drinks at beach bar Banys Verge del Carme *(p51).*

PLATJA DEL GARRAF
Entrance via Garraf Station, El Garraf;
///establishing.avocados.barging

A gorgeous secluded cove bounded by green-and-white-striped beach huts awaits after a short train ride from Barna. With some of the cleanest waters, and overlooked by the mountains of the Garraf Massif, Platja del Garraf feels a world away from the hubbub of the city. It's a quiet retreat, where dog walkers track up and down the beach, their dogs skipping in and out of the water, and couples walk hand-in-hand on sunset strolls.

BANYS DEL FÒRUM
Entrance via Parc del Fòrum, Fòrum; ///globe.brief.prestige

Okay, this one technically isn't a beach but for those who hate the feeling of sand in their clothes, Barcelona's saltwater lido is a happy alternative. Time your arrival for sunset, when this urban expanse of concrete blocks and solar panels makes for a strangely beautiful, dusky scene. The summer-only lido is cast in the Mediterranean Sea so you might even see a couple of octopuses or turtles swim past as you enjoy an evening dip.

PLATJA DEL PRAT

Entrance via Passeig de la Platja, El Prat; ///panels.sitting.myth;
www.elprat.cat/la-platja

On days off, friends pile into convoys of cars or jump on the Prat Exprés bus. Their destination? The never-ending sand dunes of this laidback outpost. It's a far cry from Barcelona's famously busy beaches, where row upon row of sun-soakers lie like sardines. Here, expanses of golden sand and a nature reserve form a lovely backdrop for a day-long party on the beach.

PLATJA DE SANT SEBASTIÀ AND PLATJA DE SANT MIQUEL

Entrance via Passeig Marítim, Barceloneta;
///verge.mailer.rugs

We've all thought it: city life can be stressful. Sometimes you just need to let your hair down and hang loose. On such days, clothing-optional Sant Sebastià, a stone's throw from the city, is just the ticket. Having trouble finding a spot? Prefer not to bare all?

Try it!
BEACH CLEAN

Tourism ravages Barna's beaches, especially those of Barceloneta. Do your part on a Saturday morning and join a beach clean. You'll likely make some friends along the way (*www.cleanbeachinitiative.org*).

No fear: you get two beaches in one here in Barceloneta. Stroll along the sand to sister beach Sant Miquel for a restorative blast of sea air with slightly different views.

» Don't leave without pausing for thought at the Som i Serem Ciutat Refugi memorial, which honours the refugees who have died in their attempt to cross the Mediterranean to find a new home.

PLATJA DE LA MAR BELLA

Entrance via Passeig Marítim del Bogatell, Poblenou;
///singles.respond.imitate

Created around the time of the Olympics, Mar Bella is Barna's de facto LGBTQ+ beach, replete with its own "BeGay" beach bar. Prepare for a lot of nakedness – Mar Bella is also one of the city's nudist beaches (when it comes to beach days, Catalans love to get their kit off). Your birthday suit isn't compulsory, mind, so you're more than welcome to keep your swimwear on. You do you.

PLATJA D'OCATA

Entrance via Passeig Marítim, Masnou; ///transmitted.wink.replace;
www.masnou.cat

A bright, sunny day and crisp paperback are all it takes to persuade urbanites to journey to Ocata, just outside the city. They sprawl out on the sand and languidly watch the waters lap along the picture-postcard beach, no *guiris* in sight. Sounds good, doesn't it? And it's definitely worth the extra 20 minutes on the train to reach it.

City Squares

Barcelona's squares are cornerstones of their **barris.** *It's in these public spaces that neighbours chitchat, friends rendezvous and grandparents watch the world go by.*

PLAÇA DE LA ROSA DELS VENTS

Map 5; access via Passeig de Joan de Borbó, Barceloneta;
///identity.hiding.madness

Ask a local what they think of the W Hotel and they'll either tell you it's an iconic point on the city skyline or a total eyesore. The one thing that everyone agrees on, though, is that the square behind the hotel is utterly idyllic. Looking out onto the Mediterranean, it's the perfect place to park up with pals and watch the sun slip behind the horizon.

SUPERILLA PARLAMENT/BORRELL

Map 3; Carrer del Parlament, 39, Sant Antoni;
///liners.secret.tweeted

Barcelona's progressive mayor Ada Colau is on a mission to make Barna more sustainable. Under her guidance, the city council has been tackling carbon emissions by closing roads around the city's grid system and opening up pavement space for the community.

Experience the *superilla* (superblock) scheme for yourself at the crossing of Carrer Comte Borrell and Carrer del Parlament. Here, old boys battle it out at the public chess tables, parents sip *orxatas* as their children let off steam and home workers enjoy a much needed break away from their screens.

PLAÇA DELS ÀNGELS

Map 2; Plaça dels Àngels, Raval; ///caveman.themes.daily

Barcelonans of all ages can be spotted commuting around the city by skateboard, or stopping for coffee with a board tucked under their arm. There are various skateparks dotted around the city but the hub of skate culture is Plaça dels Àngels, more commonly known as "Plaça del MACBA". Skaters take advantage of MACBA's expanse of concrete, drops and steps, all to an audience of appreciative onlookers.

JARDINS DE RUBIÓ I LLUCH

Map 2; Carrer de l'Hospital, 56, Raval; ///players.fixated.bombard

When the intensity of Raval is a bit much, seek sanctuary in the tranquil Jardins de Rubió i Lluch. Set around a trickling fountain, this pretty walled square is favoured by students from the nearby Massana art school and those stopping for a breather en route to MACBA. In summer, the square runs a free book exchange, so you can select a scintillating novel to read under the square's fragrant orange trees.

» Don't leave without calling in at the square's café El Jardí *(px)* for a cooling beer or cocktail.

PLAÇA DE LA VILA DE GRÀCIA
Map 4; Plaça de la Vila de Gràcia, Gràcia; ///stadium.bakers.salsa

If there's one thing that Barcelonans love to do of an afternoon, it's chill out at a pavement café with friends and a couple of *canyes*. When it comes to choosing a square for such an occasion, Gràcia locals are spoiled for choice but Plaça de la Vila takes some beating. With its pretty chiming clock tower and numerous cafés, this lovely spot is the perfect setting to quaff a glass of beer and let the conversation flow freely.

PLAÇA DEL SOL
Map 4; Plaça del Sol, Gràcia; ///hoot.slipped.behaving

Gràcia has a reputation as Barcelona's hippie hub and nowhere embodies this better than Plaça del Sol. A bohemian crowd sit on the ground in the centre of the square, strumming guitars and sketching the scene around them. Join them at it – or swap the hard concrete for the comfort of a nearby pavement café.

» Don't leave without picking up a book at the square's charming second-hand bookshop, Saturnàlia.

PLAÇA DE SANT FELIP NERI
Map 1; Plaça de Sant Felip Neri, Gothic Quarter;
///squeezed.scout.swept

On weekdays, at 5pm, tiny Plaça de Sant Felip Neri suddenly fills with the excited clamour of school kids swarming out of the school on the square, all chuffed to be heading home or to an *orxateria*.

The rest of the day, this medieval courtyard – sandwiched between the cathedral and city hall – remains quiet. It's eerie and haunting, like it's clinging to the past tragedies witnessed here. After all, the buildings of this little square are pockmarked from Civil War bombings. There's no drinking in this square; this is the place for some meditative time alone.

PLAÇA DE SANT AGUSTÍ VELL

Map 1; Plaça de Sant Agustí Vell, Born;
///hilltop.letters.discrepancy

Part-square, part-promenade, Sant Agustí Vell stretches from the Santa Maria del Mar church to the Old Born Market. During the day it's the passing place of Barcelona's hoi polloi, all busy running errands and going hurriedly about their business. When night falls, the place transforms. Punters pause at the square's bars, spilling out onto the cobblestones where they nurse glasses of wine under the streetlamps.

PLAÇA DEL PI

Map 1; Plaça del Pi, Gothic Quarter; ///averages.adjusted.nuggets

City squares don't get more charming than this spot in the Gothic Quarter. At its heart is the Basilica de Santa Maria del Pi, which watches protectively over the locals scoffing tapas in the square below. Twice a month, patrons leave their seats for the Catalan food market that sets up shop here, filling their bags with cheese, wine and chocolate and chatting to the stall owners like old friends.

Outdoor Activities

The 1992 Olympics inspired a long-lasting relationship with keeping fit. And what better place to exercise than outdoors? The temperate climate here makes this a year-round reality.

ESPIGÓ DEL GAS

Map 5; entrance via Passeig Marítim de la Barceloneta, Barceloneta; ///fracture.receive.suckle

Barna is big on giving locals space to work out for free. Take this breakwater with its own outdoor gym, where fitness fanatics work on their strength and toning, all the while keeping cool in the sea breeze. Get here early in the morning to avoid the crowds and, more importantly, the blistering heat.

INERCIA ROLLERBLADE RENTAL

Map 5; Carrer de Roger de Flor, 10, Ciutadella; ///managers.arching.fade; www.inercia.com

Make like it's the 90s and don your Rollerblades, or rent a pair from Inercia for a few euros. Weave your way round the Ciutadella park *(p176)*, through the oh-so-cool Barceloneta neighbourhood and all the way down to the locals' favourite blading spot: the

Join a free yoga classes at Parc de la Ciutadella on Saturday mornings. Don't forget your mat!

seafront promenade. Here you'll find the paved, palm-tree-lined shoreline (perfect for beachside blading) and lots of places to stop for a refreshing fruit juice.

PARC DE L'ESPANYA INDUSTRIAL

Map 6; entrance via Carrer de Muntades, Sants;
///overtime.marked.lion

Ever heard of *pilota*? Locals can't get enough of this Basque/Valencian handball sport. It's a little bit like squash, but instead of using a racket to hit a ball against a wall (called a *frontón*) you use your hands. The best spot for a game of *pilota*? Otherworldly Parc de l'Espanya Industrial could have been plucked from a sci-fi film, and offers a one-of-a-kind *frontón* setting. Those looking for a more familiar sport, rest assured: there's also basketball courts and table-tennis tables here.

» Don't leave without cooling off on the bleachers and admiring the amazing views of the artificial lake.

BARCELONA BEACH HOUSE

Map 5; Carrer del Taulat, 137, Poblenou; ///jungle.competent.poem;
www.barcelonabeachhouse.com

What could be more relaxing than saluting the sun to the sound of breaking waves? Barcelona Beach House is just the place for some much needed zen, holding English-language yoga classes near Mar Bella beach *(p167)*. Haven't packed your mat? No problem: you can rent one for the session.

Solo, Pair, Crowd

Chasing a new PB? Looking to workout with your bestie? Prefer to pair sport with a little refreshment? Barcelona's got an activity just for you.

FLYING SOLO
A run with a view

Head up to the mountains for a jog along the Carretera de las Aigües. This lovely running route stretches out along the city and winds its way through small wooded areas, promising incredible views – just what's needed to keep you going.

IN A PAIR
Soulful surfing

Grab your bestie and head down to Surf House Barcelona to find your feet on a paddleboard. Debrief on your adventure with a healthy(ish) brunch in the California-style surf shack after.

FOR A CROWD
Table tennis tournament

You'll spot ping pong tables across the city – locals are obsessed. Challenge your friends to a championship over a few drinks at Càmping (p157).

PISCINA MUNICIPAL MONTJUÏC

Map 3; Avinguda Miramar 31, Montjuïc; ///lamps.rejoin.career

Those wanting to relive the glory years make like Olympians at the summertime diving pools up on Montjuïc. They swim lengths with the city as a stunning backdrop, then it's time to dry off in the sun with a few poolside card games. Who said workouts were hard?

» Don't leave without having a well-earned snack at the Salts (p159) above the swimming pools.

SKATEPARK MAR BELLA

Map 5; entrance via Passeig Marítim del Bogatell, Poblenou; ///hears.lure.moguls

Yes, Raval is the city's skateboarding centre but those preferring to practise their tricks and flips without an audience make a beeline for this dedicated skatepark. Not only is the park's giant bowl and wave ramp more chilled but the setting is more scenic.

UNGRAVITY SUP & SURF

Map 5; Carrer de Sevilla 78, Barceloneta; ///exams.rational.renders; www.ungravityboard.com

Anyone expecting an epic surf session will leave Barna disappointed – the Med doesn't always deliver the best waves. The city is the perfect place, however, for first-timers, especially on Barceloneta beach, where the good folk of Ungravity SUP & Surf offer surf lessons. Prefer to try your hand at something a little less exhausting? Ungravity also runs stand-up paddleboarding sessions.

Parks and Picnic Spots

The Mediterranean sun lures locals out to Barna's (surprisingly few) parks and gardens. This is what life here is all about: lazy afternoons and picturesque settings, ideally with a few treats to nibble on.

PARC DEL LABERINT D'HORTA

Map 6; entrance via Passeig dels Castanyers, Horta; ///rich.relaxing.wants

Cascading waterfalls, stone-cut balustrades, a garden maze; this place is, in a word, magical. It's the domain of loved-up couples, giggling their way around the maze; oh, and the odd wild boar that's known to get lost here. The couple of euros to get in is worth it but, if money's tight, come on Wednesdays or Sundays when entry is free.

PARC DE LA CIUTADELLA

Map 5; entrance via Passeig de Pujades, Born; ///tuned.snippet.twigs

Looking for the heart of local life? You've found it. Ciutadella is the people's park and, heck, are the locals fond of it. Families hotfoot it to the boating lake, couples hitch up shaded hammocks, buskers bang on bongos and friends have a kickabout.

JARDINS DE LARIBAL & TEATRE GREC

Map 3; entrance via Passeig de Santa Madrona, Montjuïc;
///composed.lookout.nurture

The labyrinthine Jardins de Laribal is the park of choice for some romantic escapism. Dreamy-eyed locals meander under the park's wisteria-heavy pergola, past the trickling fountains before sketching the fairy-tale-like landscape from the park's steps.

» Don't leave without visiting the amphitheatre, which looks ancient but, like the gardens, was built for the 1929 International Exhibition.

MUHBA TURÓ DE LA ROVIRA

Map 6; entrance via Carrer de Marià Labèrnia, El Carmel;
///grace.geology.pickles

Known to locals as the "bunkers", this site was used by the Republican army during the Civil War. Choosing this specific spot was clearly a no-brainer: the views across the city and out to sea are second to none. Perch yourself atop the bunkers, where you'll be joined by influencers posing endlessly on the graffiti-splashed concrete.

JARDÍ BOTÀNIC HISTÒRIC

Map 3; entrance via Avinguda dels Montanyans, Montjuïc;
///slides.jigsaw.leap; www.museuciencies.cat

We know, Barna can be uncomfortable in summer. That's why a lot of locals schlep to this old quarry, which was given back to nature in the 1930s. Home to waterfalls, ponds and the city's tallest trees, the park guarantees cooler climes. Top tip: bug repellent is a must.

JARDINS DE JOAN MARAGALL

Map 3; entrance via Avinguda dels Montanyans, Montjuïc;
///veal.stacks.barmaid

Not many realise there's a royal palace with a perfectly manicured garden hidden on Montjuïc. Dotted with classical-style sculptures and grand water features, Jardins de Joan Maragall is open for just a few hours at weekends. The silver lining? Savvy souls have the place to themselves, save for a few newly engaged couples on photoshoots.

ANELLA OLÍMPICA

Map 3; entrance via Avinguda de l'Estadi, Montjuïc;
///nimbly.clean.defender

On the prowl for a picnic spot with a difference? Look no further than the retro-futurist park where all the Olympic magic went down. Wander through the Olympic park before setting up camp under Santiago Calatrava's bright-white communications tower.

» Don't leave without getting your fill of Olympic trivia at the Museum of Olympics & Sport (p119).

JARDINS DE MOSSÈN COSTA I LLOBERA

Map 3; entrance via Carretera de Miramar, Montjuïc;
///part.unlucky.browser

The green space that launched a thousand Instagram posts, Barna's cactus and succulent garden is a favourite with certain 20-somethings perfecting their social feeds. Stuffed-full of spiky desert plants and swaying palm trees, the garden also has some dreamy sea views.

Liked by the locals

"Montjuïc is my go-to when I need
to get away from the city. It's got
everything you need: the Olympic
park for sunset, gorgeous gardens,
big parks for birthday picnics and
plenty of space to stretch your legs
on a mini hike with sea views."

ALMUDENA LOZA,
PRODUCER AT PROFESSOR FILM

Nearby Getaways

Barcelonans adore their city but when the mercury rises and tourists trickle in, a change of scene is the perfect antidote. Luckily, Barna has various tempting day trips right on its doorstep.

SANT CUGAT DEL VALLÈS

30-minute train from Plaça de Catalunya station; www.santcugat.cat

Just over the mountains from Barna lies the sleepy medieval town of Sant Cugat. Locals make their way to the town's craft and vintage haven of Mercantic, ideally at the weekend when things rev up with live music and food trucks. Rummaging through the warehouses' nooks and crannies, hunting for treasure, a drink in hand – life could be worse.

GIRONA

45-minute train from Sants station; www.girona.cat

Game of Thrones fans will recognize Girona as the Free City of Braavos; gourmands, on the other hand, think of it as the crème de la crème of the foodie world (local restaurant Can Roca has twice been listed as the best in the world). And Barcelonans? It's the perfect weekend getaway, that's what. Sitting at the foot of the Pyrenees, the medieval gem is laced with cobbled streets, ancient balconies and a truly enchanting Jewish quarter. Looking to wow someone? A partner? Your parents? Girona won't let you down.

>> Don't leave without devouring an ice cream, decorated with things like burned meringue and flaked almonds, from Rocambolesc Gelateria.

TARRAGONA

1.5-hour train from Sants station; www.tarragonaturisme.cat

Sure, Rome is impressive but Tarragona is spectacular. Founded by the Phoenicians, the city was the Roman capital of the Iberian Peninsula. The result? Historic sites left, right and centre, including an amphitheatre perched right by the sea. But Tarragona is so much more than a relic. Glorious beaches, cosy bars and the Santa Tecla festival, when the streets are packed with *castells* (human towers), keep the city fresh.

SANT POL DE MAR

50-minute bus from Estació del Nord bus station; www.santpol.cat

Ask any local where to head for a chilled beach getaway and they'll say Sant Pol de Mar. This hilly fishing village is pure charm, with its cobbled lanes, *Modernista* buildings and blue waters. Better still, the sandy coves of Roca Grossa are a mere 2 km (1 mile) away – perfect for a secluded skinny dip before an evening feast.

» Don't leave without having dinner at La Casa Nostra, a Sicilian restaurant set in a gorgeous 19th-century house by the beach.

EL PENEDÈS

45-minute train from Sants station; www.penedesturisme.cat

Cava gets a bad rap, living in the shadow of its Champagne and Prosecco cousins, but Catalans remain loyal to the sparkling wine produced on their patch. City slickers embark on day trips down to Vilafranca or Sant Sadurní d'Anoia in the Penedès region, where cava hails from. Join them as they hike through the verdant countryside and vineyards, rounding off their walk with an obligatory bottle of bubbly.

Try it!
CYCLING WINE TOUR

Want to really earn that glass of cava? Take a self-guided cycling wine tour with Penedès Ecotours. You'll learn all about the wineries of Vilafranca and the art of cava-making (www.penedesecotours.com).

SITGES

40-minute train from Sants station; www.visitsitges.com

It's a classic with locals and visitors alike. So, no, you might not be alone as you zip down the coast to Sitges. Barcelonans looking to make merry after a long week at work can't resist the town's waterfront restaurants, crafty boutiques and welcoming queer bars. Prefer to while away your stay on the pristine beaches? Expect company in the form of fragile good-timers having an alfresco siesta.

FIGUERES

1.5-hour train from Sants or Passeig de Gràcia stations;
www.figueres.cat

It's all about one man, and one man only, in the town of Figueres: local boy Salvador Dalí. Admirers of the surrealist artist call in at the Dalí Theatre-Museum, a wacky red castle crowned with giant eggs (of all things), which houses over-the-top, experiential exhibitions. Truly devout fans pay their respects at the crypt, where the artist lays at rest.

MONTSERRAT

1-hour train from Plaça Espanya station; www.montserratvisita.com

There are two types of pilgrim at Montserrat: Catalan *abuelas* and thrill-seeking mountaineers. The former queue up to kiss "La Moreneta", a sacred statue of the Virgin Mary held in the Benedictine monastery that clings to the Montserrat mountains. No queuing for the climbers; they're busy clambering up the striking mountain face, motivated by the view (and picnic) that awaits at the summit.

Parc de Collserola

**Enjoy the views from
THE TEMPLE OF
THE SACRED HEART**

Circle the striking 20th-century
church and take in the incredible
views. Got the afternoon to kill?
Pop to the amusement park
next door for thrills and spills.

3

TIBIDABO

*In 1957, Walt Disney
offered to buy* **Tibidabo
Amusement Park** *for
whatever price was
named. The park
refused.*

Norman Foster's
Torre de Collserola
*communications tower
was built for the 1992
Olympics and became
an emblem of the city.*

VALLVIDRERA

4 **Sate your hunger at
CAN MARTÍ**

Peckish? Stop for a well-
earned lunch at Can Martí.
The homely restaurant plates
up Mediterranean fare along
with more fabulous views.

CARRER DEL BOSC

Built in 1904, the
Observatori Fabra *is
the world's fourth-oldest
functioning observatory.
Asteroids and comets
are studied here.*

5

**Head back down to
PEU DEL FUNICULAR**

Stroll downhill to Peu de Funicular
where the *ferrocarril* train will take you
on a short ride back into town.

RONDA DE DALT

BONANOVA

PASSEIG DE LA BONANOVA

0 metres   500

0 yards   500

VIA AUGUSTA

SARRIÀ

SANT GENÍS
DELS AGUDELLS

RONDA DE DALT

ELS
PENITENTS

**Walk along
AVINGUDA DEL
TIBIDABO**
Start your ascent on
this leafy avenue; you'll
pass pretty mansions as
you climb up Tibidabo.

TIBIDABO

2

1

**Grab coffee at
CAFÈS GENER**
Caffeine is essential
today. Stop in at
Cafès Gener for a
coffee to-go.

RONDA DEL GENERAL MITRE

A morning's hike on
Mount Tibidabo

Tibidabo takes its name from the Latin phrase, *tibi dabo*, or "I will give to you". Legend has it that the devil said these words to Jesus atop this hill, the highest of the Collserolas at 512 m (1,640 ft), as he gestured to the kingdom below. Tibidabo has long provided an escape from the city; an amusement park was built here in the early 20th century, and the hill's inclines are popular with hikers. Join them on the path for a couple of hours' walk.

1. Cafès Gener
Passeig de Sant Gervasi, 59,
Sarrià-Sant Gervasi;
www.cafesgener.com
///offers.even.goggles

2. Avinguda del Tibidabo
///rises.chickens.replied

**3. The Temple of the
Sacred Heart**
Carretera de Vallvidrera
al Tibidabo, Tibidabo;
934 17 56 86
///purest.shade.subject

4. Can Martí
Passatge de la Font del
Mont, 4, Tibidabo;
www.noucanmarti.com
///partner.puzzles.physical

5. Peu del Funicular
///forced.assorted.securing

📍 **Observatori Fabra**
///talents.unfair.napped

📍 **Tibidabo Amusement
Park** ///target.referral.mile

📍 **Torre de Collserola**
///priced.think.emperor

With a little research and preparation, this city will feel like a home away from home. Check out these websites to ensure a healthy, safe stay in Barcelona.

Barcelona
DIRECTORY

SAFE SPACES

Barcelona is a diverse and inclusive city but should you ever feel uneasy or crave community there are spaces that cater to different backgrounds, sexualities and genders.

www.acathi.org
A nonprofit association supporting LGBTQ+ migrants and refugees.

https://ajuntament.barcelona.cat/lgtbi
Barcelona's online and in-person LGBTQ+ centre, providing information, advice and direct assistance for those in the community.

www.ccicbcn.com
A cultural centre providing support and information for and about the Muslim community in Barcelona.

www.fundacioibnbattuta.org
A community centre offering social and employment support to migrants.

www.hostelle.com
A stylish and affordable female-only hostel in Horta-Guinardó.

HEALTH

Healthcare in Spain isn't free to all so make sure you have comprehensive insurance; emergency healthcare is covered by the European Health Insurance Card for EU residents and the UK Global Health Insurance Card for those from the UK. If you need medical assistance, there are many pharmacies and hospitals.

www.bcncheckpoint.com
A sexual health centre primarily aimed at gay men and trans women.

**www.catsalut.gencat.cat/ca/
centres-sanitaris**
*A search engine for types of care and
medical centres in Barcelona.*

www.clinicbarcelona.org
*Barcelona's most important university
hospital, caring for sexual assault victims
and emergency patients.*

www.farmaguia.net
*A directory of all the 24-hour
pharmacies in Barcelona.*

www.turoparkmedical.com
*A private medical centre specializing
in care for foreign patients.*

TRAVEL SAFETY ADVICE

Before you travel – and while you're
here – always keep tabs on what's
happening in Spain. Here are some
useful websites to help keep you safe.

www.aemet.es
*Weather forecasts and advisories,
including extreme temperature alerts.*

**https://ajuntament.barcelona.cat/
guardiaurbana**
*The website of the city's municipal police
force (the Guàrdia Urbana), providing
assistance in the case of an incident.*

www.mossos.gencat.cat
*Online crime reporting for Catalunya's
police force (Mossos d'Esquadra), plus a
list of police stations in the city.*

www.spth.gob.es
*The latest coronavirus-related
requirements for travelling to Spain,
directly from the government.*

ACCESSIBILITY

Barcelona is always improving when it
comes to accessibility, but some of its
winding medieval streets and old
infrastructure can prove tricky for
wheelchair users. Here are some
useful websites and resources.

www.barcelona-access.com
*Barcelona's official page for accessible
tourism, listing hotels, cultural sights,
activities and specialist agencies suitable
for those with accessibility needs.*

**www.tmb.cat/en/barcelona/
accessibility-mobility-reduced**
*A list of metro stops specifying ease
of accessibility.*

**www.turismeperatothom.
catalunya.com**
*A resource of sights and activities with
good accessibility across Catalunya.*

INDEX

ABOUT THE ILLUSTRATOR

Penguin
Random
House

Mantas Tumosa

Creative designer and illustrator Mantas moved from his home country of Lithuania to London back in 2011. By day, he's busy creating bold, minimalistic illustrations that tell a story – such as the gorgeous cover of this book. By night, he's dreaming of adventures away, catching up on the basketball and cooking Italian food (which he can't get enough of).

Main Contributors Harri Davies, Teresa Gottein Martínez, Thom Lampon-Masters, Sofía Robledo, Sam Zucker
Senior Editor Lucy Richards
Senior Designers Tania Gomes, Ben Hinks
Project Art Editor Ankita Sharma
Editor Elspeth Beidas
Designer Jordan Lambley
Proofreader Kathryn Glendenning
Senior Cartographic Editor Casper Morris
Cartography Manager Suresh Kumar
Cartographer Ashif
Jacket Designer Tania Gomes, Jordan Lambley
Jacket Illustrator Mantas Tumosa
Senior Production Editor Jason Little
Production Controller Samantha Cross
Managing Editor Hollie Teague
Managing Art Editor Sarah Snelling
Art Director Maxine Pedliham
Publishing Director Georgina Dee

First edition 2022
Published in Great Britain by Dorling Kindersley Limited,
DK, One Embassy Gardens, 8 Viaduct Gardens,
London SW11 7BW, UK
The authorised representative in the EEA is
Dorling Kindersley Verlag GmbH. Arnulfstr.
124, 80636 Munich, Germany
Published in the United States by DK Publishing,
1745 Broadway, 20th Floor, New York, NY 10019, USA
Copyright © 2022 Dorling Kindersley Limited
A Penguin Random House Company
22 23 24 25 10 9 8 7 6 5 4 3 2 1

A CIP catalog record for this book is available from the British Library.
A catalog record for this book is available from the Library of Congress.
ISSN: 1542 1554
ISBN: 9780 2415 6815 6
Printed and bound in China.
www.dk.com

MIX
**Paper from
responsible sources**
FSC™ C018179
www.fsc.org

This book was made with Forest Stewardship Council ™ certified paper – one small step in DK's commitment to a sustainable future. For more information go to www.dk.com/our-green-pledge

A NOTE FROM DK EYEWITNESS

The world is fast-changing and it's keeping us folk at DK Eyewitness on our toes. We've worked hard to ensure that this edition of Barcelona Like a Local is up-to-date and reflects today's favourite places but we know that standards shift, venues close and new ones pop up in their place. So, if you notice something has closed, we've got something wrong or left something out, we want to hear about it. Drop us a line at travelguides@dk.com